Management Education in India

Issues and Concerns

P. Satyanarayana
Lakshmi Mantha
C. Sesharatnam

SHIPRA

₹ 1250; US$ 50
ISBN: 978-93-88691-25-3

First Published in India in 2019

Management Education in India: Issues and Concerns

Published by:
SHIPRA PUBLICATIONS
LG 18-19, Pankaj Central Market
I.P. Ext., Patparganj, Delhi 110092, India
Tel.: +91 11 2223 5152/6152 , 9650028065
E-mail: info@shiprapublication.com
www.shiprapublication.com

Contents

1
Importance

Management is a relatively new concept. The term in English lexicon evolved sometime in 16th-17th century taking cue from Latin, 'Manus', Italian 'Manegiare', and French 'Management'. All the terms that preceded 'Management' implied control over others, in order to get things done or decide about how to use available recourses. Management, if performed with a sense of service to the community, can be one of the noblest professions. It can create growth, wealth and development in the society.

Indeed, 'Management' is a modern construct that gained significance during the most useful centuries in Europe marked by renaissance reforms, scientific revolution, industrial revolution, mercantilism and above all entrepreneurial spirit. Gradually, a body of knowledge developed around the concept of 'Management' although contributions came from diverse academics disciplines, such as Sociology, Psychology, Economics, Accounting, Mathematics and Law. Then Management education began in the early 20th century.

Management is the science and art of organising the components of an organisation in order to get success through the work of planning, organising, staffing, directing and controlling. The study of these components individually or jointly called study of Management or Management study. Study of Management does not only indicate to manage the various components of an organisation, it also combines well with accounting, finance, marketing, information system, human resource, operation, and supply chain. Study of Management not only needed for managers, but also it is equally important for all people who are involved in the organisation.

The study of Management is important for various reasons for developing countries. In developing countries, business and industries are gradually growing up. So far their successful management and to supply quality employees in such organisation, Management study becomes more fruitful. These countries are constructing various developing programmes and making various policies. So to consult the government managerial experts are required. It is important to study Management in order to work as an employee or become employee to run successful organisation. For developing countries study of Management should be their concern.

Management is taught as an academic subject at secondary level in many countries. At pre-tertiary level, it is called Business Study and usually combines elements of accounting, finance, marketing, human renouncement and economics. At the university level, students have the opportunity to take undergraduate degrees in Business and Management.

Why Management Education Necessary

Why management education is necessary? Following points justify the value that management education can add:

1. *Getting to Know How the Business Works:* During the study of Management course, you learn a great deal about the pillars of business. When you get into management course, you get the exposure to develop and improve your business knowledge and learn various tools and techniques. This becomes valuable in the later career which requires more analytical thinking to identify and tackle business challenges. Even for the entrance examination, many of these management institutions require them to develop real life skills, such as numeric ability, data interpretation, language skills, logical reasoning and current affairs. The graduates from the management institutes are prepared for life and have a higher success rate dealing with the upcoming life challenges.
2. *Leadership Skills get Improved:* In a Management college, you get the opportunity to come out of your cocoon and face the crowd, even if it is a challenge for you. Various seminars, workshops, projects and case-studies; enable individuals to improve their people management skills. As you progress in your career, you would need to manage people where the interpersonal skills become indispensable to grow into an effective leader. It also provides the students a valuable opportunity to explore their likes and dislikes, as well as their many talents to make the most of the upcoming opportunities.
3. *Getting Acquainted with Corporate Etiquette:* The Management students are required to undergo a few Internship Programmes as a part of their curriculum, in which they get the chance to interact with the corporate world. In the course of their internship, they get a taste of the business world, where they learn the nuances of running a business and becoming a professional. This prepares them for the real life work conditions, which sometimes may make demands, such as meeting targets, negotiating, insane working hours, people and their temperaments, pressure, and work-life balance. This ensures that the students graduating from these courses do not live in their fairy world and do not have any illusions about the harsh world out there.

4. *Learning the Management Jargon:* When you are doing your Management courses you come across management jargon, which are usually a vital part of the business world. This aids in helping a student settle sooner when they join a workforce into an organisation. In fact, knowing the management jargon help the students to easily be on the same page with their colleagues and bosses, when they have a real job. They won't feel like an alien in the corporate world. They also develop awareness about the world of commerce and it helps them out, when they are looking out for opportunities. Most of the companies are looking for employees, who can see the bigger picture and can come up with the ideas that can take the organisation forward. The Management graduates may have an edge in this regard.
5. *Better Opportunities in the Job Market*: Almost all Management colleges have a placement cell, which is dedicated to screening companies to come for campus interviews. This saves the students from visiting different organisation in search of a job. Getting a job in today's economy can prove to be a difficult endeavour and any help one gets in this regard is a blessing. The placement cells also take the students through various employability skills training sessions, which improves their chances of getting selected in the companies. It is also observed that due to the business acumen these students develop, companies are comfortable taking them at a higher salary and hierarchy than non-management graduates.
6. *Better Career Progression:* With a Management degree, getting a better designation becomes easier. The easier progression of their career can be attributed to the skills developed during their management study. Many companies find it much easier to hire the Management graduates, who are seen as already possessing the effective Management skills and not having to be taught everything from the scratch. The companies may also have policies requiring a person to be already educated in a Management course before promoting them as a manager. This is done to ensure that the promoted person has got the right skills in place to perform well in the job. Some people who are eyeing Management titles may also consider taking a sabbatical and pursuing a Management degree or going for a distant learning Management course.
7. *Starting their own Business:* The Management education also prepares you to become a successful entrepreneur. As the students become more reliant on their skills to manage the business, they may also choose the entrepreneurial path. This is especially useful for millions of students who do not want to make their career doing a regular job and would like some more freedom in their work. Students learn the real life skills of sales and finance as well as aspects of

human resource management which are all highly relevant to any budding business owner. The management education also aids them in making better business plans and approaching financial institutions and investors with their ideas.

There are many benefits of a student going for a higher education in the field of management. It can really change the individual's life by making them more efficient, focused and even ambitious. The skills learnt in the classroom of a management institute can be relevant throughout the life. The individual may find it easier to approach new avenues in life and seek out their true calling leading to a more fulfilling life and career.

Business Degrees

These include:

- The Bachelor of Business Administration (BBA) degree
- The Bachelor of International Business Economics (BIBE) degree
- The Bachelor of Commerce (B. Com. or B. Comm; Bachelor of Commerce and Administration (BCA)
- The Bachelor of Business (B. Bus.)
- The Bachelor of Management and Organisational Studies
- The Bachelor of Business Science (Bus. Sc.)
- The Bachelor of Accountancy (B. Acy or B. Acc or B. Accty)
- The Bachelor of Economics (B.Ec, B.Econ)

Postgraduate Degrees

These include:

- Master of Accountancy/Master of Professional Accountancy (M.Acc., M.Acy/MPA or M.P.Acc)
- Master of Bioscience Enterprise (M.Bio.Ent)
- Master of Business Administration (MBA)
- Master of Business and Management (MBM)
- Master of Business Education (MBE)
- Master of Business (M.Bus.) and Master of Commerce (M.Com)
- Master of Computer Information Systems (MCIS)
- Master of Economics (M.Econ/M.Ec)
- Master of Engineering Management (MEM)
- Master of Enterprise (M.Ent)
- Master of Science in Finance/Master of Applied Finance (M.Fin)
- Master of Health Administration (MHA)
- Master of International Business (MIB)
- Master of Management (MM)
- Master of Management Co-operatives and Credit Unions,

- Master of Marketing Research (MMR)
- Master of Nonprofit Organisation (MNO or MNPO)
- Master of Project Managements (MSPM or MPM)
- Master of Public Administration (MPA)
- Master of Real Estate (M.Sc.RE)
- Master of Science in Business Administration in Computer Information System (MSBA-CIS)
- Master of Science in Management (MSM)
- Professional Science Masters (PSM)
- Master in Sustainable Business (MSB)

Doctoral Degrees

These include:

- Doctor of Business Administration (DBA)
- Doctor of Commerce (D.Com)
- Doctor of Health Administration (D.H.A.)
- Doctor of Management (D.M., D.Mgt)
- Doctor of Public Administration (DPA)
- Ph.D in Management (Ph.D)
- Ph.D/M.B.A (double degree)
- Fellow Programme in Management (FPM)
- Engineering Doctorate (EngD)

Various Positions Available for Management Graduates

There are many career options available for Management graduates. Below are some of the positions that Management graduates acquire after their Management education.

1. Account Executive

- Benefits Manager
- Business Analyst
- Buyer
- Human Resources Manager
- Market Research Analyst
- Operations Manager
- Promotions Manager
- Portfolio Manager
- Media Planner
- Sales Analyst
- Training Specialist
- Purchasing Agent
- Transportation Director

2. *Who employs Management Graduates?*

- Consulting Firms
- Banks
- Advertising Firms
- Consumer Goods Manufacturers
- Market Research Organisations
- Insurance Firms
- Government
- Non-prom organisations

Skills Developed by Management

- Communication
- Analysing Ideas
- Critical thinking
- Presenting information clearly
- Organisational skills
- Project Management
- Problem solving
- Accountability
- Teamwork
- Research

Careers in Management

- Consulting
- Entrepreneurship
- Human Resources
- General Management
- Non-Profit (N GO)
- Operations Management
- Strategic Planning

Management Education Overview

Management education has been traditionally focusing on analytical models and theoretical frameworks. It is constantly under pressure to make it relevant and suited to handle and the rate at which industry is changing today. Academic rigour is not always practically relevant and hence there is a need to balance scientific enquiry and professional practice. Rakesh Khurana in his book "From Higher Aims to Hired Hands" argues that B-Schools have failed to live to their lofty ideals of educating far-sighted moral business leaders and are producing myopic career technocrats. One of the main reasons for this is the gap between the academics and industry.

The growing gap between management education and industry practice is due to the lack of mutual understanding between the two. Quantitatively, management education is growing at a very fast rate but the quality of a substantial proportion of the graduates lies far behind unable to cope with changing industry patterns. One of the main reasons for this is disconnect between the industry and the institutes and with the addition of more and more institutions combined with the limited efforts to close the gap, the situation only worsens. Across the globe, faculty members of various B-Schools realise this growing disconnect between the practice of managing and what is taught in, class. Mintzberg explains from his vast experience that there is too much of a disconnect between the practice of managing and what happens in classrooms intended to develop those managers. Many faculties around the globe also share the same experience.

Institutional Chronicle: Notable Firsts

- 1759 – The Aula do Comercio in Lisbon was the first institution to specialise in the teaching of accounting in the world. It provided a model for development of similar government-sponsored schools across Europe, and closed in 1844. Therefore, the Aula do Comercio paved the way for business schools to start.
- 1819 – The world's first business school, ESCP Europe was in Paris, France. It is the oldest business school in the world and now has campuses in Berlin, London, Madrid, Paris, Torino, and Warsaw.
- 1855 – The Institut Superieur de Commerce d'Anvers (State funded) and the Institute Saint-Ignace – Ecole Speciale de Commerce et d'Industrie (Jesuits education) were founded in the same year in the city of Antwerp, Belgium. After getting university status in 1965 and after almost 150 years of business education and rivalry between each other, both merged in 2003 into what became the University of Antwerp.
- 1857 – The world's first public business school, Budapest Business School was founded in Budapest in Austria-Hungary as the first business school in Central Europe.
- 1868 – The Ca' Foscari University was founded in Venice. It is the oldest business school in Italy and one of the oldest in the world.
- 1871 – Rouen Business School which has merged with Reims Management School under the name of NEOMA Business School. Rouen Business School is the second oldest French business school.
- 1871 – The ESC Le Havre was created (now École de management de Normandie). Created the same year than Rouen Business School it is also the second oldest French business school.
- 1881 – Wharton School of the University of Pennsylvania is the United States' first business school. HEC Paris (The École des Hautes Études

Commerciales de Paris) was established by the Paris Chamber of Commerce (CCIP).

- 1892 – The ESC Lille in northern France, which has merged with CERAM Business School (created in 1963) under the name of Skema Business School since 2009.
- 1898 – On the west coast Haas School of Business is established as the College of Commerce of the University of California with Carl Copping Plehn as the Dean in 1898 and became the first public business school. The Booth School of Business, The University of Chicago Booth School of Business also traces its beginnings to 1898, when university faculty member James Laurence Laughlin chartered the College of Commerce and Politics.
- 1898 – Handelshochschule Leipzig, today Leipzig Graduate School of Management, was founded as the first Business School in Germany, so it is the oldest university teaching economics in German speaking regions.
- 1898 – The University of St. Gallen established the first university in Switzerland teaching business and economics.
- 1900 – The first graduate school of business in the United States, the Tuck School of Business at Dartmouth College, was founded. The school conferred the first advanced degree in business, specifically, a Master of Science in Commercial Sciences, the predecessor to the MBA.
- 1902 – The Birmingham Business School of University of Birmingham is the United Kingdom's first business school. Established as the School of Commerce in Birmingham, United Kingdom. 1903 – The Solvay Brussels School of Economics and Management of Universite Libre De Bruxelles is the Belgium's first business school created by an entrepreneur Ernest Solvay, founder of the chemistry company Solvay.
- 1906 – The Department of Commerce was founded as part of McGill University in Montreal, Quebec, Canada, eventually developing into the Desautels Faculty of Management.
- 1906 – The Department of Commerce was founded as part of McGill University in Montreal, Quebec, Canada, eventually developing into the Desautels Faculty of Management.
- 1906 – The Warsaw School of Economics (SGH) was established as the first university in Poland dedicated to teaching commerce and economics.
- 1907 – HEC Montréal is founded in Montreal, being the first School of Management of its kind in Canada. It was also the first school in North America to be awarded the 3 most prestigious accreditations (AACSB, AMBA, EQUIS), which less than 70 schools in the world have achieved.

- 1907 – ESSEC Business School in Paris, which was later the first Business School outside North America to be accredited by the AACSB (main and most famous association to accredit schools of business) in 1997
- 1908 – Kellogg School of Management was founded as North-western University's School of Commerce.
- 1908 – Harvard Business School was founded at Harvard University. It was the first programme in the world to offer the Master of Business Administration degree.
- 1909 – Stockholm School of Economics was founded on the initiative of the Swedish business sector and is the oldest business school in Sweden. Hanken School of Economics was established the same year in Helsinki, Finland.
- 1914 – MIT Sloan School of Management was founded in MIT (as Course XV - Engineering Administration)
- 1919 – Babson College was the first business school founded to focus solely on entrepreneurship. Every graduate receives a Bachelor of Science in Business Administration.
- 1920 – Kelley School of Business was founded as Indiana University-Bloomington's School of Commerce and Finance.
- 1920 – First doctoral programme in business was offered at The University of Chicago Booth School of Business.
- 1936 – The Norwegian School of Economics (also known as NHH) is the oldest business school in Norway.
- 1946 – The Thunderbird School of Global Management, then called the American Institute for Foreign Trade, was the first graduate management school focused exclusively on global business.
- 1949 – The University of Pretoria in South Africa founded the oldest business school in Africa. In January 2008, the Graduate School of Management was formally replaced by the Gordon Institute of Business Science.
- 1949 – XLRI – India's oldest business management school is founded.
- 1953 – IISWBM is the first institute in India to offer an MBA degree.
- 1954 – The Faculty of Management Studies (FMS), University of Delhi is among one of the oldest business schools in India.
- 1955 – The Institute of Business Administration, Karachi was the first business school to be established outside North America to offer an MBA degree.
- 1963 – ESAN University Graduate School of Business in Lima, Peru was the first Graduate Business School founded in Latin America. It was established under an agreement between the Government of the United States of America, Stanford Graduate School of Business and the Government of Peru.

- 1991 – The IEDC-Bled School of Management was the first business school to offer an MBA programme in Eastern Europe.
- 1994 – CEIBS (China Europe International Business School) was the first business school in China to have received funding from a foreign government, namely the European Commission.
- 2001 – ISB (Indian School of business) is a private business school with campuses in two states of India, one in Hyderabad, Telangana and one in Mohali, Punjab.
- 2015 – The Daniels College of Business was the first business school to launch a challenge-driven MBA programme.

2
Evolution

The eve of India's independence in 1947 brought the hopes and dreams of a new nation. It also brought into the limelight two schools of thought propagated by some of the most prominent personalities involved in the freedom struggle. The India of Mahatma Gandhi's dreams resided in self- sufficient villages while Pandit Jawaharlal Lal Nehru, the first Prime Minister of independent India, dreamt of a modern, industrialised nation. In a letter to Pandit Nehru dated October 5, 1945, Mahatma Gandhi wrote:

> "I am convinced that if India is to attain true freedom, and through India the world also, then sooner or later the fact must be recognised that people will have to live in villages, not in towns; in huts, not in palaces. Crores of people will never be able to live at peace with each other in towns and palaces. They will have no recourse but to resort to violence and untruth".

On the other hand, Pandit Nehru's vision was, "we cannot stop the river of change or cut ourselves adrift from it and psychologically; we, who have eaten the apple of Eden, cannot forget the taste and go back to primitiveness". When Pandit Nehru was the Prime Minister (1947-1964), he laid a foundation for the technical and management education in the country to realise his vision of making India a technically advanced nation.

In the initial years of its inception, the discipline of management was viewed with scepticism in India. It was only after the deliberate efforts of academicians involved in management education and after the absorption of the first few batches in the industry that management courses started to become popular. Over time, a variety of institutions that were diverse in their visions, mission, structure, governance and scale of operation, started offering courses in management. By the 1990s, the skepticism associated with the discipline was replaced by a sense of 'elitism' and post liberalisation in 1991, the number of institutes multiplied rapidly. However, the multiplication of institutes that lack a proper infrastructure and resources stimulated a debate on the quality of management education in the country. Currently, management education in India is at a crossroads of having to deal with a large number of institutions on one hand and practical problems like a shortage of resources and declining quality on the other hand.

A brief account of management education in India is presented here in order to understand origin of management education, establishment of different institutes and landmark events that have shaped the present management education system in the country.

Key Role

Management education has a vital role to play in today's business environment, where everything changes so fast that it makes it difficult for organisations to survive the growing competition. This has led to the need for business schools in developing nations to impart relevant education to students, which reflects the changes in the society.

Management education in recent times has received enormous attention and gaining importance in India. The economic liberalisation, globalisation, industrialisation and privatisation over the past decades are few of the important reasons for gaining importance of management education. However, the challenges in management education are manifold in terms of institution building, enhancing the educational quality, covering global perspectives, developing ethical standards, seeking industrial collaborations and developing eastern perspectives in the management thought.

Management education adds value to the existing qualifications. It enhances managerial and leadership skills by sharing of ideas, insights through healthy meaningful and case study discussions. Having students with cross cultural backgrounds value to management education, as there is probability of generating multiple ideas. Apart from providing requisite skills and abilities to get going smoothly of the corporate world, it provides an opportunity to network with others and promises cross cultural diversity. It helps in equipping the executives with competencies and capabilities to take on the corporate challenges with confidence.

Time Line

Business education has a long history in India, dating back to the 19th century. Early Business-Schools were focused on the commercial side of business, seeking to fulfill the needs of the then British government.

- India's first B School i.e., Commercial School of Pacchiappa Charties was set up in 1886 in the southern city of Chennai (Madras).
- In 1903, British government initiated Secondary school level commerce classes at the Presidency College in Kolkata with a focus on Secretarial practice, Business Communication, Short hand, Typing, Correspondence and Accounting.
- The first college level Business School was founded in 1913, in Mumbai i.e., Sydenham College.

- Soon followed by another college in Delhi, in 1920 as Commerce College, later on it was renamed as Shri Rama College of Commerce.
- The Indian Institute of Social Science founded in the year 1948 as India's first management programme with an intention to train manpower to create and spread the knowledge, required for managing industrial enterprises in India.
- Catholic community founded Xavier Labour Relations Institute (XLRI) at Jamshedpur in 1949.
- Indian Institute of Social Welfare and Business Management (IISWBM) was set up in 1953 at Kolkata. That was considered as India's first official Management Institute.
- Encouraged by the results, Government of India applied for and obtained grant from the Ford foundation in 1961 to launch two (2) Indian Institutes of Management, one at Kolkata (West Bengal), and other at Ahmedabad (Gujarat). This grant was focused on helping American Business education knowledge and models to other nations and having intensive collaboration with an American B-Schools for facilitating the transfer of learning.
- IIM-Kolkata established in collaboration with the Sloan School of Management (MIT) for faculty and pedagogy development in the year 1961, with an intention to focus on Quantitative and Operational aspects of management.
- IIM-Ahmedabad was founded in 1962, pioneered the case method of teaching in India with an emphasis on Qualitative strategic-integration.
- The mission of IIMs was to professionalise Indian Management education through teaching, research, training, institution-building and consulting with the support of expertise developed by the pioneering IIMs.
- Two more IIMs were founded in Bengaluru (Karnataka) and other in Lucknow (U.P.) in 1973.
- The Indian Institute of Forest Management was setup in 1982 in Bhopal (M.P.) as a leader in specialised management education for the entire forestry system in India with the help of IIM-Ahmedabad.
- In late 1990's, two more IIMs were setup, one at Kozhikode (Kerala) and the other at Indore (M.P.).
- Growth both in numbers and status occurred during the 1990's. A large number of multinational companies entered in India. Domestic companies also followed to compete with multinational corporations. Companies found that the graduates from commerce stream fell considerably short of the demands of the executive positions in a competitive world. They had good accounting skills but lacked requisite marketing, behavioural, finance and operations skills. They

were also weak in oral and written communication, critical thinking and critical reading skills and in Information technology. Consequently, rather incurring on training cost for commerce graduates companies started offering huge premiums for MBA graduates. Recognising the success of MBA programmes and demands from students and employer, universities started looking at management education as an academic discipline and started offering MBA and BBA programmes.

The early 1990s showed a boom of founding new management schools, most of them are in private sector. Few B-Schools have also being established in collaboration with some western universities.

Management education in India is in the phase of change. The two current developments sweeping India, namely liberalisation and globalisation have had a considerable impact on management education. Today, there are several B- Schools in the country, spread over in different states of India.

Present Structure

The present structure, divided into six categories, is as follows:

1. Indian Institutes of Management (IIMs) setup by Government of India.
2. University Departments of Management studies, distance, correspondence and part time courses as well.
3. Colleges and institutes affiliated to universities.
4. Private or Govt. Institutes approved by All India Council for Technical Education (AICTE).
5. Private Institutes or colleges not affiliated to any universities are not approved by AICTE.
6. Private colleges or Institutes offering MBA courses in India in collaboration with foreign universities, where degree and diploma certificates are awarded by the foreign universities.

History

Decade	*Event*
1940s	First management institute XLRI, started few courses in management (1949)
1950s	Short-term programmes by MIT and AIMA
	First full time management programme started by IISWMB (1953)
	3 years part-time post graduate management programme in DSE, University of Delhi (1954)
	First diploma programme for public senior executives started by IISc (1954)
	Diploma in business management, DMS, University of Madras (1955)
	Management training by IIPA (1954), ASCI (1956) and NPC (1958)
	Prof George Robbins, University of California invited by Ford Foundation (1959)

1960s	IIMC and IIMA set up (1961) NITIE for engineers (1963) Full time management programmes in JBIMS, University of Bombay (1965) MONIRBA, Allahabad University (1965), FMS, Banaras Hindu University (1968) Department of Commerce and Business Management, now UBS, Punjab University (1968)
1970s	IIMB set up (1972) DIME, IIT-Kanpur (1974) School of System and Management Studies, IIT Delhi (1976) MDI, Gurugram (1973), SIBM, Pune (1978), IRMA, Anand (1979), LIBA, Chennai (1979)
1980s	IIML set up (1984) IMT, Ghaziabad (1980), TAPMI Manipal (1980), KISIM, Mumbai (1981), IMI, New Delhi (1981), BVB's SPJMR, Mumbai (1981), IBS, Hyderabad (1985), BMIT, Greater Noida (1988)
1990s	DMS, IIT, Delhi (1993) VGSoM, IIT, Kharagpur (1993) Management school in IIT, Bombay (1995) renamed as SJMSoM (2000) DoMS, IIT, Roorkee which was then University of Roorkee (1998)
2000s	189 institutes set up on an average every year from 2000-2006

AIMA Journal of Management and Research, May 2015

Growth from 1958-2012

Year	*Number of Management Institution in India*
1958	9
1968	14
1978	58
1988	87
1998	682
2000	744
2005	1052
2006	1132
2007	1149
2008	1523
2009	1940
2010	2262
2011	2385
2012	2450

Courses

Since inception different nature of courses in management education are developed like Certificate, Diploma, Bachelor Degree, PG Diploma, Master Degree etc. And in addition to this Bachelor of Business Administration (BBA), Bachelor of Business Studies (BBS) and Bachelor of Business Management (BBM) are the courses introduced at graduation level. Post Graduate Diploma in Business Management (PGDBM). Post Graduate Diploma in Management (PGDM), PGDDRM and PGDHEM are few prominent diploma courses degree generation. Master of Business Management (MBM) and Master of Business Administration (MBA), Master of International Business (MIB), Master of Management Programme (MMP), Master of Performance Management (MPM), Master of Personal Management (MPM), Master of Business Studies (MBS) are the courses at master degree are given through entrance exams MAT (Management Aptitude Test), GMAT (Graduate Management Aptitude Test), CET (Common Admission Test), ATMA, E-MAT, XAT, CEMAT, OPENMAT, IIFT (IIFT entrance test for IIFT, New Delhi and Kolkota), BIMTECH etc are conducted in India.

The Master of Business Administration (MBA) attracts from the wide range of academic disciplines. The core courses in the MBA programme are designed to introduce students to the various areas of business, such as accounting, finance, marketing, human resources, operations management, etc. Students in MBA programmes have options of taking general business courses throughout the programme or can select specialisation areas. Accreditation bodies exist specifically for MBA programmes to ensure consistency and quality of graduate business education. Business school offers MBA programmes tailored to full-time, part-time executive and distance learning students' specialised concentrations. The education in management develops capabilities like presentation skills, team building capabilities, problem solving skills etc.

Master of Business Administration (MBA) courses are of two years and divided into four semesters, and subjects taught in all the four semesters relates to management education like Accounting for business Decisions, Economic Analysis for Business Decisions, Legal Aspects of Business, Business Research Methods, Organisational Behaviour, Basics of Marketing, Marketing Management, Financial Management, Human Resource Management, Management Information Systems, Strategic Management, Enterprise Performance Management, Start-up and New Venture Management, Information Technology, Operations Management, Human Resource Management, International Business Management, Supply Chain Management, Rural and Agri-business Management, Managing for Sustainability, subject core courses in Marketing and Finance.

However, during the second year, students can select a special subject, from the different areas like Marketing Management, Financial Management,

Computer Management, Production and Materials Management, Human Resources Management and nearly 8-0 specialised disciplines are developed, based on the need.

Overseeing Agencies

Department of Higher Education, MHRD: The Ministry of Human Resource Development has two departments – Department of School Education and Literacy and the Department of Higher Education. The latter department works for the planned development of higher education through 100 autonomous bodies including the UGC, AICTE,IIMS,IITs etc.

All India Council for Technical Education (AICTE): The All India Council for Technical Education (AICTE)was set-up in November 1945as a national level Apex Advisory Body to conduct survey on the facilities on technical education and to promote development in the country, in a coordinated and integrated manner. As stipulated in the National Policy of Education (1986), AICTE was vested with statutory authority for planning, formulation and maintenance of norms and standards, quality assurance through accreditation, funding in priority areas, monitoring and evaluation, maintaining parity of certification and awards and ensuring coordinated and integrated development and management of technical education in the country.

Board of Management Studies under AICTE: The AICTE Act confers the power on the council to constitute the Board of Management Studies. It advises the Executive Committee of the Council on academic matters falling in its area including norms, standards, model curricula, model facilities and structure of courses (AICTE Act, 1987).

National Board of Accreditation (NBA): NBA was setup by the AICTE in September 1994 for the purpose of assessment of Quality and Accreditation of Technical programmes in India. The major objective of NBA is to encourage the institutions to continually strive towards the attainment of excellence. The NBA evaluation process is designed to facilitate identification of the strengths and weaknesses of the programmes under accreditation. The process is based on a set of eight broad-based criteria developed through a lengthy participatory process involving more than 1000 participants concerned with Technical Education all over India. Institutions seeking accreditation of their programmes are expected to satisfy each of the criteria individually. They are expected to adhere to these criteria during the validity period of accreditation granted. They are also encouraged to periodically review the strengths and weaknesses of their programmes and strive for their continuous improvement.

*University Grants Commission (UGC):*The UGC was formally established only in November 1956 as a statutory body of the Government of India through an Act of Parliament for the coordination, determination and maintenance of standards of university education in India and thus, affects the management education delivered through university departments.

All India Management Association (AIMA): Founded in the year 1957,All India Management Association (AIMA) is an apex body of management with over 30,000 individual members, 3000 institutional members and 60 Local Management Association across India and overseas created with support from government and industry. AIMA undertakes a host of management related activities and initiatives, such as Distance Management Education, Management Development Programmes, Special Conferences, Research and Publications, Testing Services and Competitions.

Current Issues

In a research paper published in *International Journal of Business and Administration Research Reviews* (Jan-March 2015) current issues in Indian Management Education are identified. These are:

1. Preach-practice gap
2. Industry-institute co-operation
3. Quality of the faculty
4. Quality of faculty development programmes
5. Changing role of institutes
6. Accreditation of institutions
7. Value orientation of business management graduates
8. Admitting students without work experience
9. Issues related to placement

Concerns of Management Education

At present we have more than 5000 Business Schools. While supply has risen to meet the fast-growing demand, lack of quality has left the graduate with mere degree but no career. To make the Indian MBA graduates more employable, Management Institutions need to "make a conscious effort to bridge the gap between the academia and industry that is theory and practice".

HR managers from 10 companies in Hyderabad were interacted to understand the present quality of management graduates. The Managers perceived that the following attributes were lacking in students:

1. Technical skill
2. Passion/interest in career development
3. Analytical skills
4. Communication skills
5. Awareness about industry
6. Career decision-making skills
7. Flexible/adaptable attitude

8. Problem solving skills
9. Awareness about career options
10. Application of knowledge
11. Goal setting
12. Values and ethics
13. Business knowledge
14. Learning skills
15. Enthusiasm

Academicians perceived that the following skills were lacking in the students:

1. Communication skills
2. Technical/domain skills
3. Language skills
4. Learning aptitude
5. Ethics
6. Leadership skills
7. Team building skills
8. Time management skills
9. Etiquette
10. Decision-making skills
11. Critical thinking skills
12. Lateral thinking skills

Directions for Future Development

At present management education is grouped along with engineering technology, pharmacy and architectural education, all of which come under the classification of technical education. This does deserves appear to be a logical grouping in the current scenario, management education deserves to be seen, handled and directed as a separate system. The AICTE norms, which are currently in vogue have grown out of the criteria which were developed way back in 1964. They are needed to be revised according to the changing needs. The AICTE should take a look at the norms and standards recommended by the AIMS. Many management institutions are not following the norms of AICTE, where no action has been initiated to control them. Hence, a proper mechanism needs to be developed to take disciplinary action on them. All the management institutions, should maintain good infrastructure including classrooms, conference halls etc., by using latest technologies like LCD teaching methods etc. The composition of faculty composition with a significant number should be with retired experts. The student-teacher ratio as prescribed by AICTE and UGC, should be strictly followed. Further research in management education should be initiated at the post graduate level itself to make the students learn about the practical problems before they actually enter into the industry. Also, the doctoral and post-doctoral research in management education should be concentrated hard by identifying new and emerging areas. In this millennium, the Indian Management education is undergoing a major transition Internationalisation, cross cultures, strategic alliances, partnership and mergers are the new trends in management education. So, the Indian management education system should also concentrate in this direction.

Global Standards and Ensuring Quality

It is important that management institutions in the nation adopt and follow the global standards of education and incorporate the following in their infrastructure and pedagogy:

- Make management education student centric not faculty centric
- Involve in industry collaboration to hone up the practical skills of the students via internship/training
- Organise regular practical training at a related management industry to help the students capture to right pulse
- Craft the management curriculum in line with the latest industry trends, standards and practices
- Incorporate digital education, which is a must in the current scenario, whether to train students or the faculty
- Have faculty with diversified experience. Gone are the days, when the faculty used to remain restricted to just teaching. Today they should diversify to training, research, and consultancy.
- Engaging students in seminars etc. where industry experts impart them with current knowledge
- Globalise education: This can only be done by collaborating with foreign universities. India's upgraded education policy will go a long way to help do this
- Replace most of the theory-based education slowly yet steadily with practical-based education as only this comes handy, when the students look for jobs in corporate world outside
- R&D based collaboration: Constant research and development, whether in the industry or its related education, is a must and thus, it is important that the curriculum at a management school keeps updating with the changing demands of the industry. This can be achieved only when a management school collaborates with the bigwigs of the industry to walk hand-in-hand to create world class management graduates/post graduates.

Top Business Schools in India

Indian School of Business (ISB), Hyderabad: The Indian School of Business (ISB) was founded in 2001 by two senior executives from McKinsey and Company. It is a private school. Even though, it is the first business school in India to be accredited by the Association to Advance Collegiate Schools of Business (AACSB), ISB is not accredited by the Indian statutory body, the All India Council for Technical Education (AICTE), as it has chosen not to apply for the accreditation.

ISB has been ranked 33rd in the world in the 2015 Financial Times Global MBA Rankings.

Indian Institute of Management, Ahmedabad (IIM-A): Indian Institute of Management, Ahmedabad has consistently been ranked as the number one management school in the country year-after year-in the last several years. In its latest ranking, the Economist has ranked IIMA at 56 among the top 100 international B-Schools in the world that offer full-time MBA. The Financial Times (FT) has ranked the two-year post graduate programme in management (PGP) of IIMA in the top ten programmes in the category of Masters Programmes in Management that do not require work experience as pre-requisite for admission. FT reported that this was the first time that any Indian B-School was not only included in the survey but also achieved such high ranking.

The Financial Times has also ranked the one-year post graduate programme in management for executives (PGPX) among the top MBA programmes globally. The two post graduate programme in management with a specialisation in agri-sector (PGP-ABM) is ranked at number one among comparable programmes globally by Edu-universal.

*Indian Institute of Management, Kolkata (IIM-C): T*he Indian Institute of Management, Kolkata (IIM-C) was established as the first national institute for Post-Graduate studies and Research in Management by the Government of India in November 1961, in collaboration with Alfred P. Sloan School of Management (MIT), the Government of West Bengal, The Ford Foundation and Indian industry.

Over the years, IIM-C has grown into a mature institution with global reputation, imparting high-quality management education. It has been playing a pioneering role in professionalising Indian management through its Post Graduate and Doctoral level programmes, Executive Training Programmes, Research and Consulting Activities.

Indian Institute of Management, Bengaluru (IIM-B): IIM-Bengaluru (IIM-B) is the third IIM to be established after IIM-Ahmedabad and IIM-Calcutta (Now Kolkata). It was founded in 1973. IIM-Bengaluru has the distinction of being situated in India's Silicon Valley, which is a notable advantage as compared to almost all the other IIMs. IIM-B offers Post Graduate programmes, Doctoral Programme/FPM as well an Executive education programme.

Xavier Labour Relations Institute of Management (XLRI), Jamshedpur: XLRI – Xavier School of Management is a leading management school based in Jamshedpur, Jharkhand, India. Established in 1949 as the Xavier Labour Relations Institute, XLRI is acknowledged as India's oldest business management school. The Jesuit managed school's main programmes include a full-time 2-years post graduate programme in Business Management, Personnel Management and Industrial Relations (re-christened as Human Resources Management in 2011) and Global MBA, 15 months full-time General Management programme (PGDM-GM), doctoral fellow programmes (FPM) and many executive education programmes.

Indian Institute of Management, Lucknow (IIML): The Indian Institute of Management, Lucknow was the fourth one to be established by the Government of India back in 1984. It has a satellite campus in Noida for its executive programmes, and is ranked among the top business schools in India .IIM-L is recognised as an "Institution of Excellence" by the Ministry of Human Resource Development, Government of India.

Faculty of Management Studies (FMS), Delhi: Faculty of Management Studies (Commonly known as FMS, Delhi), established in 1954 under the aegis of the University of Delhi, offers management education to the professional managers as part-time and full-time MBA programmes. It is one of the oldest business schools in India which started offering a Full-Time MBA programme.

FMS is known for its academic programmes, training programmes, research, and consultancy, but its primary aim is long-term academic programme leading to a Degree Certification.

Currently, FMS conducts the following long-term programmes:

- MBA (Full Time)
- MBA(Executive)
- MBA(Executive)Health Care Administration
- Doctoral Programmes
- Bachelor of Management Studies

In addition to all these programmes, FMS also regularly conducts Management Development Programmes.

Indian Institute of Management, Indore (IIM-I): The Indian Institute of Management Indore (often abbreviated as IIM-I) is an autonomous public business school located in Indore, Madhya Pradesh. Instituted in 1996, IIM-Indore is the sixth addition to the prestigious Indian Institute of Management (IIM) family of management schools.

IIMI offers following academic programmes:

- Integrated Programme in Management (IPM)
- Post Graduate Programme in Management (PGP)
- Executive Post-Graduate Programme in Management (EPGP)
- Post Graduate Programme in Management for Executives (PGPMX)
- Fellow Programme in Management (FPM)

Indian Institute of Management, Kozhikode (IIM-K): The Indian Institute of Management Kozhikode is one of the 13 Indian Institutes of Management set up by the Government of India. The Institute, founded in 1996, in collaboration with the State Government of Kerala, was the 5th IIM to be established.

IIMK offers following academic programmes:

- Post Graduate Programme in Management
- Fellow Programme in Management
- Executive Post Graduate Programme
- Social Development Initiatives
- International Exchange

S. P. Jain Institute of Management and Research (SPJIMR), Mumbai: S.P. Jain Institute of Management and Research (SPJIMR) is a constituent of the Bharatiya Vidya Bhavan and is recognised as one of the premier business schools of India. The Institute grew rapidly in eminence from one of the three B-Schools in Mumbai in 1981 to one of the top ten B-Schools in the country by 1994-1995.

S.P. Jain offers following academic programmes:

- Post Graduate Diploma in Management
- Post Graduate Programme in Management
- Executive Management Programme
- Family Managed Business Programme

Jamnalal Bajaj Institute of Management Studies (JBIMS), Mumbai: Jamnalal Bajaj Institute of Management Studies (JBIMS) was established in 1965 by University of Mumbai in collaboration with the Graduate School of Business of Stanford University. It is Mumbai University's Department of Management Studies and has been named after the noted industrialist and philanthropist, Jamnalal Bajaj.

Tata Institute of Social Sciences (TISS), Mumbai: Originally established in 1936 as the Dorabji Tata Graduate School of Social Work, TISS is regarded as India's first school of social work. The institute originally offered postgraduate diploma in Social Work. However, over the years TISS has expanded its outlook considerably to offer courses in policy, planning, action strategies and human resource development. Currently, TISS has four campuses in Mumbai, Tuljapur, Hyderabad and Guwahati.

Indian Institute of Foreign Trade (IIFT), New Delhi: The Indian Institute of Foreign Trade (IIFT) is an autonomous public business school established in 1963 by the Government of India to help professionalise the country's foreign trade management and increase exports.

Its flagship programme is the Master of Business Administration in International Business (MBA-IB). It is the only institute among the top-10 business schools of India that offers this programme.

Apart from the MBA (IB) Course, IIFT provides various Management Development Programmes, Executive Programmes and Certificate Programmes catering to the requirements of aspiring International Business executives and mid-career professionals alike.

Management Development Institute (MDI), Gurugram: Management Development Institute (MDI) is one of the premier business schools in India. It was established in 1973 and is located in Gurugram, a commercial hub near the Indian capital of New Delhi. Its second campus has come up near Murshidabad, West Bengal.

MDI offers following academic programmes:

- Post Graduate Programme in Management (PGPM)
- PG Programme – Human Resource Management (PGP-HRM)
- Post Graduate Programme in International Management (PGPIM)
- National Management Programme (NMP)
- Post Graduate Diploma in Public Policy and Management
- Fellow Programme in Management
- Executive Fellow Programme in Management
- Part Time Post Graduate Programme in Management (PT-PGPM)

National Institute of Industrial Engineering (NITIE), Mumbai: National Institute of Industrial Engineering (NITIE) was established in 1936 as 'National Institute of Training in Industrial Engineering' by the Government of India. It is recognised as one of the 15 Centres of Excellence by the Ministry of HRD, Government of India. NITIE is renowned as the top Indian school for operations and supply chain management.

- Shailesh J. Mehta School of Management (SJSSoM), IIT-B
- Narsee Monjee Institute of Management Studies (NMIMS), Mumbai
- Symbiosis Institute of Business Management (SIBM), Pune
- Symbiosis Centre for Management and HRD (SCMHRD)
- Indian Institute of Management, Shillong (IIM-S)
- Indian Institute of Foreign Trade (IIFT), Kolkata
- Indian Institute of Management, Ranchi (IIM-R)
- Indian Institute of Management, Trichy (IIM-T)
- Indian Institute of Management, Rohtak (IIM-Ro)
- Indian Institute of Management, Raipur (IIM-Rai)

3

Committees and Commissions

A number of committees and commissions looked into management education in India and identified the systemic issues and made suggestions for strengthening the management/business education in the country. Briefly, the suggestions of such bodies are given here.

Nanda Committee

Nanda Committee was the first committee that reviewed the working of the three Management Institutes of Management at Ahmedabad, Kolkata and Bengaluru, to make recommendations for the promotion and development of management education in India. The Nanda Committee suggested a series of measures in 1981 for strengthening management education in India, viz:

- Adequate funding for research to be provided without soliciting project funding. Consultancy research should cover both basic and applied types.
- IIMs should act as mother institutes and foster growth of other management institutes in the country.
- There is an urgent necessity to develop expertise in international management and offering of educational and training programme in international management.
- Government control should be progressively reduced, as each institute becomes more and more self-reliant.

Management education has to be research based, and utility based, the institutes should become self-reliant and the government must relinquish control over the years.

Kurien Committee

Government of India appointed a second review committee under the chairmanship of Mr.V. Kurien in 1991, to look into the direction and functioning of the four institutes of management. The committee submitted its report in 1992.The salient recommendations were:

- The mission of the Institute of Management to strengthen management in business, industry and commerce is still relevant. The mission statement, however, needs to be expanded to emphasise the IIMs' commitment to public service and public management.

- The inter-relatedness of teaching, research and consulting needs to be better emphasised for greater synergy.Choices in approving research and consultancy must be exercised to strengthen their inter-connectedness and mutuality.
- There should be a much greater emphasis on the development of relevant teaching materials and research. Appropriate polices and rewards should be initiated to strengthen this aspect of IIM functioning.
- The Government should take a flexible view in providing financial support to the different IIMs and encourage the institutes to vigorously pursue revenue generation, cost cutting, and fund raising efforts. The non-plan maintenance professional approach; but also introduced new age courses in accordance with industry demand which have more economic value in today's time. Management education is one among those, which got a new dimension with this changing time. Initially Marketing, Finance and Human Resource Management were considered as functional area of management, but now management education covers much more functional areas like Operations, Information Technology, International Business, Supply Chain Management, Retail etc. India has witness a continuing growth in this sphere of education because of the rising demand of trained management graduates. Management education has become one of the most sought after education, today as a result of this; private sector has entered in Indian Management scenario and invested an immense amount for this.

Management education in India is not very old, after the establishment of the IITs, there was dire need for similar establishment in the field of management education. Thus came into existence Indian Institute of Management, Ahmedabad (IIMA), followed soon after by one in Kolkata (IIM-C). Starting with the establishment of 4 Indian Institutes of Management Kolkata (1961), Ahmedabad (1962), Bengaluru (1973), Lucknow (1984), now management education is being offered as full time/ part time MBA programmes by some leading universities in the country. Recently and particularly during the last 4-5 years the country has witness a tremendous growth in the founding of management institutions most of them in private sector offering management programmes in different functional area of management. Concurrently, there is a mushrooming of B-Schools in the country (over 2500 institutes, of which about 1940 are certified by the All India Council for Technical Education (AICTE), leading to issues of quality.

According to annual report (2009-2010), published by the Ministry of Human Resource Development, there were 20 universities and 500 colleges at the time of independence. As on 31 December, 2009, there are 504 universities, 53 state private universities, 40 central universities and 130 deemed universities. Tables 1 and 2 shows growth of AICTE approved technical institutes. In last five years, the number of AICTE approved colleges has increased by almost 70 per cent in total in various disciplines, whereas number of management institutes has seen growth of 90 per cent in terms of number of institutes and growth of 123 per cent in terms of intake.

TABLE – 1
Growth of AICTE Approved Technical Institutions

Year	*Engg.*	*Mgmt.*	*MCA*	*Phar.*	*Arch.*	*HMCT*	*Total*
2005-06	1475	1052	976	629	118	70	4320
2006-07	1511	1132	1003	665	116	64	4491
2007-08	1668	1149	1017	854	116	81	4885
2008-09	2388	1523	1095	1021	116	87	6230
2009-10	2972	1940	1169	1081	106	93	7361

TABLE – 2
Growth of Intake in AICTE Approved Institutions

Year	*Engg.*	*Mgmt.*	*MCA*	*Phar.*	*Arch.*	*HMCT*	*Total*
2005-06	499697	80464	55548	32708	4379	4435	677231
2006-07	550986	94704	56805	39517	4543	4242	750797
2007-08	653290	121867	70513	52334	4543	5275	907822
2008-09	841018	149555	73995	64211	4543	5794	1139116
2009-10	1071896	179561	78293	68537	4133	6387	1408807

After the institutes have become financially self-supporting with the creation of the corpus fund and the package of measures for augmenting its internal resources and cutting down cost, the government grants may be limited to programmes considered high priority and of social relevance by the government including the area of public system management.

IIMs re-oriented their operation subsequent to this report. They revised the fee structure and started raising resources through industrial consulting. This helped the IIMs to become financially self-sufficient.

Ishwar Dayal Committee

Many management institutes came up between the 1995 and 2000. The Government of India appointed another committee to develop future perspectives of management education in the light of the fast changing economic, social and business environment. The main challenge in management education has been triggered by globalisation of economies, rise of market economy, rapidly changing technology and developments in communication. During 1950-1980, about 118 management institutes came up and during 1985-2000 periods 673 new institutions came up.

- Most institutes that were set up during the 90s did not follow conditions prescribed by AICTE in respect of faculty strength, library, computer facilities and the like.
- They did not promote research, development of faculty or of the teaching material.
- Due to rapid expression of teaching institutions, AICTE was unable to develop an adequate mechanism for enforcing standards.
- The teaching methodology shows inadequate concern for applying cumulative knowledge in dealing with the managerial problems.

Among all the action areas, faculty development was considered the most critical. It was propose that 8 to 10 institutions should focus on this. Though the committee gave its report in 2001, there were no major initiatives from AICTE for faculty development or development of teaching materials so far. Subsequent to this, a committee was constituted by AICTE to review management education in India.

Management Education Review Committee

AICTE appointed a committee in 2003 to come up with a policy and action plan for the development of management education in India, in the context of our current national requirements and national trends.

This committee suggested the following steps for strengthening education, viz.:

- Increase the focus on under managed sectors such as cooperatives, forestry, urban management, infrastructure, rural development, education and legal systems.
- The admission of students in management schools should be only through recognised tests organised on all India basis and used for short listing candidates for group discussions and interviews. The number of admission tests could be progressively reduced, say to two or three tests.
- Accreditation is one of the major means of assuring quality. Only 15 PGDM programmes approved by the AICTE have been accredited.

- Inspite of having excellent institutions, research output, by and large, of even the more prestigious institutions has not been adequate. This needs to be rectified. Over the next decade, research has to get its rightful place in the activities of management schools. While the accreditation process will help in improving the quality of teaching and training, it is imperative that research also figures prominently as a major element in the portfolio of activities of accredited institutions.
- In order to have a better global exposure, to suit the requirement of industry under globalisation, there is a pressing need for globalisation of management education.
- Another element, which is important for globalisation, would be to keep our country, open to the presence of foreign business schools and universalities. It is necessary for Indian institutions to work out strategies to go abroad, and allowing foreign universities to come to India, without too many obstacles.
- That there is a severe shortage of faculty in the entire technical education system is well-recognised. In management education, the problem is more acute.

National Knowledge Commission

The National Knowledge Commission (NKC) was constituted in June 2005 as a high level advisory body to the Prime Minister of India. The vision for NKC was articulated in the address of Manmohan Singh, the Prime Minister of India. The report of NKC was a compilation of the recommendations submitted by NKC till November 2007 on reforms relating to education. These include Management Education besides others. These recommendations are given below.

New Regulatory Framework: NKC advocates good governance rather than the prevalent system of a prior control being exercised by AICTE in this sphere. The current regulatory regime focuses on punitive actions rather than on nurturing institutions. NKC proposes that an autonomous Standing Committee for Management Education be set up under the Independent Regulatory Authority for Higher Education. Its main role would be to exercise due diligence at the point, it approves a license to grant degrees/ diplomas. In doing so, it would assess the academic credibility and the financial viability of the proposed institution on the basis of information submitted in accordance with the stipulated criteria. It will apply exactly the same norms to public and private institutions, just as it will apply the same norms to domestic and international institutions. It would, in addition, license agencies to take care of accreditation. Other responsibilities of the Standing Committee will be to collate as well as communicate information on Management Educational Entities (MEEs); set up an information exchange;

conduct demand forecasting of managerial manpower, and develop and maintain a low cost e-monitoring system.

Grading Institutions: The Standing Committee will stipulate grading norms and nominate independent rating agencies to assess and categorise MEEs. Mushrooming private MEEs necessitate a reliable rating system to help the market function better, enabling students and employers to compare different MEEs. Hence, a two stage rating process is recommended. In the first stage, rating covering infrastructure may be mandated before an MEE can admit students. The second stage would consist of rating of quality (admission process, teaching, research and publications) which shall be conducted every three years to ensure accountability. Grading norms for each of these steps should be established in consultation with experts. CRISIL and ICRA were consulted in the process and they have agreed to undertake rating of MEEs. The Standing Committee shall decide on a fair and transparent mechanism to deal with the conflicting points of view between a rating agency and an MEE.

Accreditation: For MEEs, which wish to go beyond rating, the Standing Committee shall determine the criteria and the processes of accreditation in consultation with experts from academia and industry. Mentoring to help MEEs sustain quality standards should be an integral part of the process. Select international accreditations may also be recognised. Branding of accreditation, similar to international standards such as ISO 9001, may be considered to encourage MEEs to pursue excellence.

Improve Access: In addition to the framework of affirmative action already in place, we suggest improving access, based on work experience and educational loans. NKC believes that management education can be made available to a much wider student community by adopting a two pronged approach. First, we suggest that more weightage be assigned to work experience in admissions. This would help in overcoming disadvantages faced by prospective students due to lack of proficiency in English. Secondly, steps may be taken to ensure easier access to educational loans through banks. Default concerns can be addressed if the respective MEE and the first employer co-operate with the banks. MEEs must also offer scholarships to socially disadvantaged students.

Social Context: It is essential to widen the scope of management studies and enhance its relevance.

- Sensitise management education to our unique socio-cultural situation by including India specific case studies in the curriculum, reflecting our diversity and incorporating traditional wisdom.
- Integrate management with other knowledge sources and increase research funding for management and supporting disciplines. With globalisation, the need for management education to pursue a wider scope and realise a more wholesome impact on society has increased.

Management departments in universities should, therefore, draw upon knowledge sources in other departments.

- Encourage MEEs to design and offer executive programmes for government officials, NGOs and defence personnel. Short-term courses for government officials will help them in their role as economic managers.
- Revamp the existing Bachelor's degree in management, the Bachelor's in Business Administration, to cater to the burgeoning need of management graduates. Compulsory apprenticeship in organisations and study of under managed sector areas should be included as part of the programme. The current bookish nature of the curriculum is not sufficient to prepare students for junior management levels.
- Distance learning has considerable potential in this domain. We, therefore, need to fully realise the potential of Online Management Programmes to bridge the demand-supply gap.

Faculty Development: Non-availability of adequate proficient faculty is a major constraint for sustainable growth of quality management education in India. An autonomous, financially sound and academically credible institute with active support from the leading management institutes, industry and Government should be set up for faculty development. Standards for curriculum covering the entire spectrum need to be set. Active involvement of MEE faculty in training, conferences, industry engagement and curriculum revision should be encouraged. Given the current demand-supply gap, additional faculty would need to be attracted by appropriate incentives.

Mentoring: To achieve excellence in the field of management, NKC recommends that all the leading Management Institutions adopt 3-4 MEEs for mentoring and upgradation of quality. Funding and other modalities can be mutually worked out between the institutions.

New Institutions: There is a need for a new wave of management institutions, which will focus on entrepreneurship, leadership and innovation. These institutions will enable to launch India in to the global arena, without the legacy associated with operating in a protected environment. These institutions should set new standards and become role models for MEEs that have the desire to become leaders in the global market place. Incentives need to be provided to Indian entrepreneurs/corporates to set up institutions of excellence on their own or in collaboration with foreign universities. We could also consider allowing reputed foreign universities to enter this field, regulations for them being at par with private institutions.

Autonomy: All existing management institutes excluding management departments in universities should register with the Standing Committee of IRAHE and be accorded independent status. In the case of MEEs set up by Central and State governments, government should be treated as a promoter.

Registered institutes will benefit from the Standing Committee's mentoring and better funding opportunities apart from other advantages associated with autonomy.

Governance: NKC recommends a board of governors for all MEEs, consisting of 50 per cent independent members, as there are independent directors under Company Law. The key focus of the governing board should be to continuously improve quality of education and research. For this purpose, they would have to maximize their source/funds inflow and allocate/spend them purposively and efficiently. The Board should encourage faculty to publish reputed journals and publications, obtain regular feedback from students on teaching-learning process, obtain recruiter feedback for improving quality, institutionalise faculty evaluation and management system and encourage faculty to write India based case studies. The appointment of Directors of public MEEs should be freed from direct or indirect interventions on part of the governments, for these should be based on search processes and peer judgment alone. Likewise, the appointment of directors of private MEEs should be based on a transparent selection process. This would ofcourse be accompanied by enhanced accountability, based on performance indicators and independent external evaluation.

Non-traditional Management Education: The need for better management in education, health, local government, co-operatives, and civil society organisations and so on has often been felt. However, the experience of graduates of Institute of Rural Management and Institute of Forestry Management shows that a lack of advancement opportunities in the Government acts as a barrier to the success of such programmes. There is a need to establish career opportunities in public management, and systematise recruitment and retention policies. Structure of fees for these courses should be formulated in accordance with earning opportunities. We also need to encourage reputed MEEs to develop specialised courses for agri-business, rural banking, public utilities, regulatory agencies and services sector in the coming years, as private players entering this space would create demand for the same. The Standing Committee should undertake a study in this field to institutionalise these programmes.

IIM Review Committee

Government of India brought the committee into being in October 2017.It submitted its report in September 2008.This is the seventh committee in the history of the IIMs and the third review committee. The terms of reference to the committee are:

1. To review the present status of IIMs in fulfilment of their objective as centers of excellence in management education and research.

2. To review the existing courses being offered in IIMs, in the light of their relevance and national priorities.
3. To review their organisational and administrative structure and to suggest suitable charges therein with a view to serve better the country's economic and social development needs.
4. To review expansion plans of the IIMs during the next decade, and particularly during the eleventh plan, with a view to optimal utilisation of the existing capacities.
5. To review the position of the corpus fund in each institute and to suggest broad guidelines for better utilisation of this fund.
6. To review the per student cost on various courses being offered by the institutes and to suggest guidelines for proportionate recovery of this cost from student fees, government grants, interest income from corpus fund etc.
7. To review and suggest measures for easy availability of educational loans to students.
8. To review availability of scholarships, fellowships, free ships and other forms of financial assistance to the students.
9. To review the incentive schemes prevailing in various IIMs for faculty and non- faculty staff and to suggest suitable modifications therein.
10. To give recommendations on the issue of powers and functions of Chairman, Board of Governors of IIMs.
11. To report on any other aspects that is relevant to overall effective and efficient functioning of these institutes.

Executive Summary of the Report

- The six functioning Indian Institutes of Management (IIMs) established over different periods, have emerged as great teaching institutions and their products are in high demand in India and abroad.
- IIMs enjoy complete academic freedom and admission to them is strictly on merit.
- One new IIM has recently started at Shillong and the Government has announced that 6 more are to be established. Bringing the new IIMs to even the level of the present IIMs would be an enormous challenge.
- IIMs have not been able to expand their admission capacity for the MBA programme (PGP) adequately, to match the rapidly rising demand both from the increased rate of growth of the Indian economy and higher world demand.
- The quality and quantity of research papers from IIMs have not been commensurate with the status of IIMs and have not enabled IIMs to become thought leaders.

- IIMs have not been able to attract enough faculty, especially in the functional areas, where there is demand from other sectors. This has inhibited growth of MBA admissions.
- The Government determined remuneration for the faculty has been a deterrent to attracting adequate faculty to the IIMs, particularly in the functional areas.
- The responsibility for the governance of IIMs is divided between the Government the Boards of the IIMs and the Directors. None of them have been able to play an effective role in developing strategies and goals for meeting new challenges, and making IIMs institutions, which could rank with the best business schools in the world.
- Divided responsibility for governance, and lack of clarity of the role of the Government, Boards, Chairman and the Directors has meant that none of the key players have any real accountability for results.
- The Directors of IIMs, because their somewhat ambiguous position between the Government and the Boards, have not also been effective in driving IIMs to greater degrees of excellence.
- IIMs are, and will to an increasing degree face intense competition from private business schools, and could lose their pre-eminent position, if remedial steps are not taken now.
- The economy and the Indian people expect IIMs to enhance their brand image, expand admission capacity for the MBA programme, become thought leaders and provide means blind education based purely on merit.

Recommendations of the Committee

1. Long-term excellence of any institution is closely correlated to the quality of governance. Good governance requires that all involved should have clarity of roles, powers to execute the allocated tasks and accountability for results.
2. IIMs have been established by the Government with public funds, are perceived as public institutions and thus, IIMs cannot expect to become fully independent of the Government.
3. At the same time, there are several limitations inherent in the Government being directly involved in framing policies and strategies, and monitoring their implementation, so that IIMs become though leaders and amongst the best business schools in the world.
4. This task would become virtually impossible, when the number of IIMs increases to 13.
5. To assist the Government in playing its role, it is proposed to create a Pan-IIM Board, consisting of 15 members. 5 of these would be the Government nominees, and the rest would be eminent and

highly successful individuals living in India or abroad, and who are willing to devote time to work on this Board. The Chairman should be nominated by the Prime Minister and the Secretary of the Board would be one of the 5 Government nominees. This Board should not be involved in any day-to-day management matters of IIM, but would approve Vision and Mission statements, give guidelines for framing policy, and approve 2 year business plans. The Board would review performance of each IIM once in two years, and would advise Government on all matters relating to the IIMs. The Government should act only on the advice of this Board.

6. The Pan-IIM Board should bring about coordination between all the IIMs in all the areas where this would be beneficial. The establishment of the 6 new IIMs should be coordinated by the Board. This Board should also help in raising private funds for the IIMs.
7. The Boards of IIMs should be reconstituted and consist of 11 members against the present 25-26.Six of these would be independent professionals. The other 5 would be one nominee, each of the Central Government, State Government faculty, and the Chairman and the Director. No person should be a Board member for more than 6 years, with a single term of 3 years. Board members would be expected to have a minimum of 75 per cent attendance.
8. A Committee-headed by Secretary, MHRD and including 3 independent professionals should make the initial selections to the Boards. Thereafter, vacancies in each Board would be filled by the Boards themselves.
9. An attempt should be made to induct as many IIM alumni as possible, both in the IIM Boards and the Pan-IIM Board.
10. The Board of the IIMs should have full powers to manage, including selecting and appointing the Director, proposing the name of the Chairman to the PAN-IIM Board, raising funds, determining fees for all courses, creating or abolishing posts, and determining conditions of service of all those appointed on a contract basis.
11. The Memorandum of Association of each IIM should be amended to implement the changes being proposed.
12. The Boards should ensure that the policy of 'means-blind' education is sincerely implemented. While bank loans would form the basis of financing education, IIMs should build an adequate scholarship fund to provide assistance in all genuine cases.A transparent and objective scheme should be formulated for providing assistance.
13. Wide publicity, on a centralised basis, should be given to this policy.
14. IIMs should sponsor and support students to procure PH.Ds, to substantially increase their availability over time.

15. To overcome the faculty shortage situation, various possibilities have been suggested, including the appointment of teachers on contract, use of technology, increasing output of Ph.Ds, and rationalising the Fellowship Programme.
16. The MBA teaching programme should remain the core activity of IIMs, with adequate quality research being carried out. Income generating executive training programmes and consultancies should be balanced with needs of teaching and research.
17. All IIMs, which are over 5 years old should be able to generate a small operating surplus. The fee for the MBA programme should be fixed after taking into account all other incomes, and the need to have a small surplus. This surplus should be used to partially fund new infrastructure, and also to build the scholarship fund.
18. IIMs should first attempt to increase annual intake for the PGP to 750.This would enable better economies of scale being achieved.
19. The Government may fund 70 per cent of all new capex in the older IIMs. The rest should be raised by the IIMs, New IIMs would need to be fully funded by the Government.
20. Raising a corpus should be a prime objective of each IIM. Some changes to the tax laws may be required. The IIMs should have flexibility to be able to use the funds so raised, above a base level of Rs.50 crores, without any Government approvals or controls.
21. Existing IIMs should be actively involved in the establishment and management of the 6 new IIMs. The brand image IIMs would be tarnished, if these IIMs do not attain the same degree of excellence as the existing IIMs.
22. The academic and administrative functions in IIMs should be separated. This would enhance efficiency and also give faculty more time to teach and so research. Much greater use of technology should be made in administrative functions.

4
Business Schools

A business school is a university level institution that confers degrees in business administration or management. A business school is an educational institution that specialises in teaching courses and programmes related to business and management, such an institutions can also be known as school of management, school of business administration or colloquially B-School. A business school teaches topics, such as accounting, administration, strategy, economics, entrepreneurship, finance, human resource management, management science, management information systems, international business, logistics, marketing, organisational psychology, organisational behaviour, public relations, research methods and real estate among others.

There are several forms of business schools, including a school of business, business administration and management.

- Most of the university business schools consist of faculties, colleges or departments within the university, and pre-dominantly teach business courses.
- In North America, a business school is often understood to be a university programme that offers a graduate Master of Business Administration degree and /or undergraduate bachelor degree.
- In Europe and Asia, some universities teach mainly business courses.
- Privately owned business school, which is not affiliated to any university.

Indian B-Schools are broadly classified as:

1. Autonomous B-Schools, which are affiliated to Ministry of HRD and ACITE, such as Indian Institutes of Management, Xavier's Labour Relations Institute, Jamshedpur, S P Jain Institute of Management and Research, Mumbai, Xavier's Institute of Management, Bhubaneshwar, Fore School of Management, Delhi etc.
2. Management schools and departments in universities come under the purview of national university education system. They are regulated and monitored by University Grants Commission (UGC), Central Universities and nominated by UGC and state universities are monitored by state governments and partially by UGC.

3. University Affiliated Colleges are guided by University rules and regulation.
4. Private Universities sponsored by societies/trusts/corporate bodies are guided by UGC.

Growth of B-Schools in India from 1950-2006

Period	*No. of B-Schools added*	*Average Annual addition*
(1950-1995) 30 years	118	4
(1980-1995) 15 years	304	20
(1995-2000) 5 years	322	64
(2000-2006) 6 years	1017	169

Source: Adapted from Dayal, I., "Developing Management Education in India", *Journal of Management Research* 2(2)

AICTE approved Management Institutes (2017-18)

1. Total institutions – 3264
2. New institutions – 48
3. Closed institutions – 23
4. Total India Enrolment – 3,94,835
5. Faculties – 55,876

There appears to be a correlation between the number of schools in a state and its economic and industrial development. The regional imbalances in development and the creation of capacity for management education in the state are probably related.

Factors Responsible for Growth of B-Schools

According to Ashutosh Priya, there are various reasons for the tremendous growth of B-Schools in India. There have been fundamental and irreversible changes in the economy, government policies, outlook of business and industry, and in the mindset of the Indian in general:

- From a shortage economy of food and foreign exchange, India has now become a surplus one.
- From an agro-based economy, India gas emerged as a service oriented one.
- From the low-growth of the past, the economy has become a high-growth one in the long-term.

- Having been an aid recipient, India is now joining the aid givers club.
- Although India was late and slow in modernization of industry in general in the past, it is now a front-runner in the emerging knowledge based new economy.
- The Government is continuing its reforms and liberalisation not out of compulsion but out of conviction.
- Indian companies are longer afraid of Multinational Companies. They have become globally competitive and many of them have become MNCs themselves.
- Indian management graduates are no longer queue up for safe government jobs. They prefer and enjoy the challenges and risks of becoming entrepreneurs and global players in the emerging private sectors.

Stable Country and Institutions

- India being a largest democracy with stable, mature, vibrant and exemplary democratic governance and institutions, boasts lots of quality B-Schools attracting intellectual students in large members every year.
- Possess strong and transparent legal and accounting system.
- There are numerous watchful and proactive NGOs.
- Free, vocal, alert and quality media. India has 5600 dailies with a combined circulation of 60 million, nearly 15,000 weeklies and 20,000 periodicals in 21 regional languages.
- Legal protection for intellectual property rights.

Common Degrees

Associate's degrees: AA, AAB, ABA, AS

Bachelor's degrees: B.com, BA, BS, BBA, BBus, BSBA, BAcc, BABA, BBS, BMOS and BBusSc.

Master's degrees: MBA. MBM, MM, MAcc, MMR, MSMR, MPA, MISM, MHA, MSF, Msc, MST, MMS, EMBA and MCom. At Oxford and Cambridge business schools an MPhil or MSc is awarded in place of an MA.

Doctoral degrees: Ph.D, DBA, DHA, DM, DCOM, Ph.D in Management or Business Doctorate, DPS.

Ranking

Each year, well-known business publications, such as *The Economist*, *Eduniversal*, *U.S. News and World Report*, *Fortune*, *Financial Times*, *Business Week*, *Expansion* and *The Wall Street Journal* publish rankings of selected MBA programmes and business schools that, while controversial in their methodology, nevertheless can directly influence the prestige of schools that achieve high scorers. Academic research is also considered to be an important feature and popular way to gauge the prestige of business schools. Business schools share the common purpose of developing global managerial talent and to this end, business schools are encouraged to accelerate global engagement strategies on the foundations of collaboration and innovation.

Time B-School Categorisation

With the objective of empowering our students with both the knowledge and understanding of the important parameters to evaluate B-Schools and helping them arrive at the right decision. T.I.M.E releases a list of India's top B-Schools annually. This list segregates B-Schools into various categories, thereby aiding the students in choosing the set of B-Schools they should apply to. This list is made using a methodology that has a proven track record of over a decade-and-a-half, after months of extensive research by experts who have over two decades of experience in guiding students on MBA admissions.

Parameters used in categorisation of lists:

- Quality of students
- Placements
- Age and image of the institute
- Location of B-Schools
- Quality of infrastructure
- Fee

B-Schools are divided into 7 broad categories:

1. Top
2. AAA+
3. AAA
4. AA
5. A
6. B+
7. B

Top 10 category features world-class institutes, like the IIMs and XLRI that every student aspires to secure an admission into. Many of these institutes are comparable with the best in the world. Indeed some of them regularly feature in the lists released by business magazines. These institutes invariably have a 100 per cent placement record. Even the not-so-academically good students at these institutes manage to get good jobs on account of the 'rub-off' effect of the institute.

Indian Business Schools

There are around 4500 business schools in India as of 2015. Some of them are even in the list of top 100 colleges of the world. But in the last two years, near about 200 business schools have been shut down and at least 120 more are on the same way.

Top B-Schools are sending their students to big companies for internships to provide them practical knowledge. With increasing internationalisation Indian B-Schools are improving a lot from the past few years. Indian B-Schools prepare students for the corporate world. They teach dressing etiquette, corporate etiquette, discussion skills, team work and much more in the course itself. Indian business schools are trying to catch up the international standards. There have been drastic improvements from the past few years. But still a lot needs to be done. We should adopt best practices in the world, and at the same time there is a need to Indianise the business education. To cater to the need of businesses, new management institutes are being set up and seats in the existing programmes are getting multiplied. There are roughly 2000 business schools in India that are churning out 100,000 management graduates. In the next 10 to 15 years, it is estimated that the demand for management professionals will grow to 300,000 graduates. While the demand will grow, the supply is likely to be of varied quality. As a result, companies and the market have started discriminating the quality of institutions and management graduates.

Distance Learning B-Schools

The emergence of Distance Learning Education System in our country, a few decades ago has been a welcome development. It indeed faced its initial phase of uncertainty. Fortunately, the wheel has turned in the right direction and now this mode of education has established its credibility, competence and capability. The education system, industry and policy-makers are now convinced that Distance Learning Education can play a crucial role in the merging educational scenario in our country.

The mode of education has undergone a transformation over years. Today, it is pragmatic and dynamic. Now it is not only confined to providing course material but also offers multimedia and technology support as well as inputs to strengthen the learning process. The highly innovative, professional and technology-enabled approaches and practices have emerged in this area of education, which has completely changed the face of this mode of education.

Since Distance Learning Education is no longer looked upon as an impediment to pursuing a course, the interest of students and several working professionals in this stream of education is growing. It has spread its roots all over the globe. It is considered to be one of the latest technologies to provide education and eligibility for employment to all, without any disparity. It is a lifetime to those who challenges, such as geographical distances or physical disabilities

Keeping this importance of distance learning mode of education in mind, we believe that it is very essential for us to highlight a few of the most reputed distance-education institutions/universities, so as to facilitate stakeholders take important career related decisions.

Here is a list of some of the well-known distance learning B-Schools in India. The list is presented in a random order. The institutes/universities mentioned in the list have embarked upon success through their unique and innovative teaching and learning methodologies.

Some of the Well-known Distance Learning B-Schools in India

Sl. No.	*Name of the Institute*
1	Prin L N Welingkar Institute of Management Development and Research, Mumbai, Maharashtra
2	IMT, Centre for Distance Learning, Ghaziabad, Uttar Pradesh
3	Directorate of Distance Education, Kurukshetra University, Kurukshetra.
4	Sikkim Manipal University, Gangtok, Sikkim
5	Lovely Professional University, Phagwara, Punjab
6	Centre for Open and Distance Learning, Tezpur University, Nappam, Assam
7	University of Petroleum and Energy Studies, Dehradun, Uttarakhand
8	ICFAI University
9	Symbiosis Centre for Distance Learning, Pune, Maharashtra
10	Amity University, Noida, Uttar Pradesh
11	NMIMS Global Access School for Continuing Education, Mumbai.
12	Annamalai University, Annamalainagar, Tamil Nadu
13	Bharathiar University – School of Distance Education, Coimbatore.
14	Dr B R Ambedkar Open University, Hyderabad, Telangana
15	MATS University, Raipur, Chhattisgarh
16	MIT School of Distance Education, Pune , Maharashtra
17	Indira Gandhi National Open University – School of Management Studies, Maidan Garhi, New Delhi
18	Alagappa University, Karaikudi, Tamil Nadu
19	Suresh Gyan Vihar University, Jaipur
20	Bharathidasan University – Centre for Distance Education, Tiruchirappalli, Tamil Nadu
21	Osmania University – Prof. G Ram Reddy Centre for Distance Education, Hyderabad, Telangana
22	Bharati Vidyapeeth University (Deemed to be University), Pune
23	Yashwantrao C Maharashtra Open University, Nashik, Maharashtra

Choosing a B-School

In the first instance, one should give serious consideration to the top B-Schools, if one is not able to secure admission, then at least the following three factors have to be kept in mind while choosing any other B-School.

First, one should be clear about the objective of joining an MBA programme. Why to do MBA? What is it that one wants to get out of the programme? Is it simply of getting a job or to acquire new skills and knowledge to pursue a career of one's choice? Or, is it to start one's own business? Motivation to join MBA programme should be clear in terms of one's aspirations and career goals. That will greatly help in deciding which B-School to join and how much efforts one has to put in for attaining the set goals.

Second, the reputation of a B-School is important. It has to be accredited or at least approved by AICTE. Apart from ranking, one may have to look into the extent of contact which the B-School has with business and industry, quality and reputation of faculty, structure of MBA programme, infrastructural facilities and quality of student life on the campus. They can consult the website of the B-School and look at the mandatory disclosure done under AICTE regulations.

Third, most of the B-Schools make exaggerated claims about placements and facilities and one may have to verify whether they are true in actual practice. For this, it is better to visit the campus and have a feel of campus environment and find out whether it is conductive to learning. Interaction either with the present students or alumni will reveal how the MBA programme helps them in their placement. It is important to find out what kind of companies continuously visit the campus, their reputation, what kind of initial salary they offer and whether enough companies visit to recruit MBA graduates in the field in which one intends to specialise.

B-Schools Admission Process

Admission process and standards differ from institution to institution. Getting accepted by a college is a big challenge. Students do not get selected in colleges based only on highest grades or test scores. There are several factors, which make a student eligible. These include special talents, personal characteristics and ability to afford costly fee colleges take into account in student's admission the following:

- The top concerns while selecting a candidate?
- What is the ideal background for pursuing MBA?
- How much weightage is given to graduation marks?
- How to prepare for GD and what?
- How to prepare for personal interview?
- What should be my budget for pursuing MBA?
- Do the marks for extra-curricular activities matter?

- How to get a loan for MBA?
- Does quality of faculty matter?
- What is the criterion to pursue an MBA aboard?

Challenges

Students Lack Experience: B-Schools in India face the problem of intake of students, which varies in quality, and students having no work experience. Apparently parents want their children to finish the post-graduate education before opting to work. Thus, students lack industry experience which is essential for management education.

Subsequently, students fail to appreciate real challenges when companies and industries are facing. To overcome this serious, lacunae management education requires a massive experimentation in terms of extended summer internship for four to six months or in terms of experiential learning, which involves several live projects of shorter duration. With students getting hands-on experience with companies and industry, they will be able to connect with the programmes in a more meaningful way.

Lack of Soft Skills: Another challenge that B-Schools face is lack of soft skills among students, which is necessary for becoming successful mangers. Many of them come from a background in the first 15 years of education, which does not prepare them for the number of soft and life skills which help them to be a better manager. So, the training for soft skills becomes an added responsibility of B-Schools to prepare the students for the tight kind of job. Making students employable from day one is the topmost challenge for B-Schools in India.

Shortage of Competent Faculty: For any B-School to impart meaningful business education, the quality of faculty members is paramount. Moreover, the faculty body with all its qualification needs to connect with the industry. Management education in India, for all its benefits, is largely disconnected with the industry. Faculty members are not doing the kind of research that is valued by companies as well as the practicing managers. Very few faculty members are actively engaged with management development programmes, consultancy and research with companies. So the knowledge shared by majority of faculty members becomes theoretical, or, borrowed from international B-School which may not be relevant to the Indian context. A few successful B-Schools have recruited faculty members, who have doctoral and research degrees, and fair amount of working exposure with companies across the industries.

Identification of Business and Social Problems: There is serious absence of a debate among management educators about pedagogy and the curriculum, which could solve the problem that India's B-Schools are facing currently. To identify India's business and social problem and to conduct research and seeking solutions for those problems remain as the foremost challenge.

Absence of Active Association with Companies, Industries, and Societies: The existence of B-Schools is highly dependent on a close as well as active association with companies, industries and societies. Many Indian companies are not organised, and not open to the idea of faculty members conducting research and writing about the issues which companies may not be comfortable with. The close collaboration of businesses and B-Schools will prove enormous value to both. Fresh ideas and new frontiers can come from B-Schools along with trained managers and staff. IRM, Anand provides that model in India and MIT Sloan School of Management and Kellogg School of North-western University and Stern NYU work in close co-operation with industries and businesses.

More Focus to Other Sectors: B-Schools have to expand their focus area to other sectors so that they become socially more relevant. Areas like public governance, sustainable development, agriculture and rural management, environmental and natural resources management, functions of municipality and local bodies and co-operatives and public sector management need to be given importance.

Need to New Design Socially Relevant Processes: In the next 10 years when a majority of the population will start living in cities, the actions of municipal corporations and local bodies will define the quality of living across Indian cities. The quality services provided by these organisations to the public have to increase qualitatively. But where are those people and ideas, which make municipalities become more efficient? B-Schools have a responsibility to promote training of managers beyond businesses. B-Schools have to provide ideas with research and to design simple and transparent processes for these institutions to remain socially relevant.

Curriculum to be Tuned to New Changes in Environment: As India is developing economically, the state of our environment is getting precarious. Rivers have high level pollution, sources of water are getting contaminated with an overdose of fertilisers and pesticides and other industrial chemicals; the amount noxious gases and particles are on a rise. Businesses which are generating jobs an wealth are also spewing harmful gases and effluents to the environment. The cost of development at the cost of environment is a scary proposition. B-Schools have the responsibility to find a way out, and to strike the right balance, where economic development does not mean environmental and cultural depletion of people and the society. Businesses have the responsibility to the sustainability of the environment. B-Schools have to come up with those ideas, and have to promote technology as well as businesses which will promote environmentally sustainable businesses, products and services. The B-Schools' curriculum and training have to incorporate this reality.

Challenges of B-Schools

Kulwant Singh Pathania and Anuradha Pathak of Himachal Pradesh University Department of Commerce and Management highlighted some of the significant challenges to quality:

- Demand for professional trained managers
- Inadequate infrastructure
- Lack of skill development in management teaching
- Lack of computer knowledge
- Inadequate quality of faculty members
- Inadequate promotion to research quality
- Faculty development programme
- Issue of students' intake
- Fake rankings and credit ratings
- Lack of practicality
- Requires experimentation

Choosing B-School

Management degree prepares us theoretically and practically for the dynamic trends that are bound to happen in any industry. With the boom of internet and related technologies, no industry is stable; disruption is happening in every industry and in some, it is lightning fast.

An MBA degree helps us with the tools, techniques and methodologies that can be applied to addressing the business problems. It helps to bridge talent gap between the young, energetic students and strategic business needs, thereby developing the Management graduates of today into business leaders of tomorrow.

An MBA aspirant should not only look for the best institution by today's standards but also need to look for the willingness and the ability of the institution to adapt to industry talent requirements. Key factors (not necessarily in hierarchical order) that should be studied while choosing a B-School are:

- Rank and accreditation among order B-Schools
- Placement record
- Level of interaction between industry and B-School
- Level of interaction between students and alumni
- Dynamic curriculum and teaching methodology
- Job related hard (domain specific skills) and soft trainings (communication skills, problem solving skills, leadership skills)
- Faculty profile – adequate and relevant work experience with respect to their domain
- Average age of board members
- Effective summer internship programmes (SIPs)

- Participation in industry conclaves and business summits
- History of B-School
- Hostel and food facilities
- Sports and cultural clubs

Challenges

- Most of the syllabus in Indian B-Schools is relevant to the developed economies of the west rather than developing economies like India.
- Though some B-Schools like IIM, IIT are competing with the global standards and all the remaining business schools are not really trying to improve their course standards.
- According to a study by the Associated Chamber of Commerce and Industry of India (Assocham), 2016 about 93 per cent of India's B-School graduates are not actually employable.
- Most of the business schools in India are facing the problems like lack of infrastructure, poor faculty, lack of research opportunities etc.,
- The Indian business schools select their students largely on the basis of marks. As long as a student has got excellent marks, he/she's in. We need managers not scholars.
- Except for roughly 2-3 per cent B-Schools, it has become business with fees rising as high as 15 lakhs and the number of students in a class being more than 200 in some colleges. Only some colleges have been providing proper attention to this problem.
- Indian MBA programmes have become placement factories.
- There is shortage of teachers at higher educational institutes. Even this is the case with the top-institutes like IITs, IIMs etc.
- A dire shortage of Ph.Ds delays in the recruitment and lack of incentives have been an important cause of the inability of the institutes to nurture the new talent.
- Problem lies not only in the higher education but from the primary education, where the low quality education results in the weak basics of the students.
- Indian B-Schools are placement oriented rather than education oriented.
- Admission to B-Schools is not that hard because of the availability of management quota. This diluted value of B-Schools.
- Over professionalisation of business is curtailing innovation.

Overcoming Challenges

How to overcome the challenges faced by B-Schools? A few suggestions are:

- Focusing on quality education not quantity
- Re-engineering the curriculum of management education

- Encourage students to take up teaching profession by providing decent salary package and ambience
- Training the present faculty members to update their skills and ability
- Students have to put through interactive, and practical sessions than mere preaching
- of text book case studies
- Exposing students to industry so they can understand the problems of the industry realm
- Provide professional training to students which focus on the current scenarios, which will groom the students take on challenges faced in the real business world
- Take action on unauthorised and illegally raised B-Schools
- Schools should focus on the teacher student ratio, which sparks individual attention

What makes a great B-School?

Be it the Nanda Committee, the Kurien Committee, the Ishwar Dayal Committee or the Management Education Review Committee, all constituted by the Government of India, have unequivocally indicated the systemic problems ailing management education in India. According to reports submitted to the government, the problems highlighted were on account of shortage of quality faculty, lack of research, and lack of industry interaction. Essentially, a great B-School must be in the business of creation of knowledge, application of knowledge and dissemination of knowledge.

Quality Faculty: For any B-School to impart meaningful business education, the quality of faculty members is paramount. The expertise of the faculties, their research publications, how instrumental are they in framing public policies, the quality of the MDPs and workshops conducted, etc., are indeed the hallmark of a great B-School. The training, consulting and advisory roles that they undertake have a direct bearing on the quality of teaching, which no longer remains theoretical, but is laced with practical inputs. The knowledge shared is not merely borrowed from international B-Schools, which may or may not have any relevance in the present domestic business context. Having said this, academicians from a particular institute, being on the board of companies and on advisory committees of the government, adds to the credibility of the institute.

However, in the Indian context, the reality is that B-Schools suffer from acute shortage of quality faculty. Given that salaries of faculty members is substantially low compared to international B-Schools and corporations, there is no incentive for talented people with a Ph.D., substantial industry experience and an academic inclination, to opt for academia. While many Indians are heading top global B-Schools, Indian B-Schools suffer from acute shortage of quality faculty.

Integrated Research: Research undertaken by a faculty or an institute is an investment that can be ploughed back into the quality of teaching, consulting and training. B-Schools must not see research as cost centers; rather it must encourage faculty members to undertake integrated research. It not only enriches the pedagogy, but also provides interface with the wider academic and corporate world. The focus on research portrays the institute as one which is focused on creation of knowledge and thought generation and sets it apart from run-of-the-mill institutes, which focus merely on placements. Integration of research and its business application also helps in having collaboration with foreign B-Schools and common research undertakings.

According to a study conducted by London Business Schools (LBS), Aditya Birla India Center Professors Nirmalya Kumar and Phanish Puranam, the research output of Indian B-Schools is nothing to write home about and compared to Asian standards, dismal; leave alone international standards. As a matter of fact, between 1990 and 2009, India as a whole contributed to only 108 papers in the top management journals, i.e. about five papers a year. It goes without saying that research is the biggest casualty in management education.

Industry Relevance: Given that the existence of a B-School is dependent on a close as well as active association with industry and society at large; management education should reflect ground realities of businesses. The corporate needs should be well echeloned in management education curriculum by emphasising more on practical exposure and execution skills as against just theory. This will help in creating an industry-ready employable workforce. To this end, faculties should have regular interaction with management practitioners and understand the business requirements and challenges. Many foreign B-Schools such as The Stern School, New York University and Indian B-Schools like ISB and IIM-A promote the idea of having industry professionals as adjunct faculties and leaders in residence; this can be the ecosystem for all B-Schools.

5

System of Total Quality Management Education (TQME)

Quality is complex issue and can have various interpretations. It can be referred to in terms of products, process and system. In the present world, when sustained development has become a watch word, the system approach to quality has gained utmost importance and relevance. Globalisation and increased domestic competition have brought a sense of urgency in introducing highly successful TQM techniques to Indian organisation and including education organisation.

Mohan and Goswami, have rightfully stated that "Quality is not an accident, it is always the result of high intention, sincere efforts, intelligent direction and skillful execution. It can be classified as an attitude or characteristic".

The concept of total quality management can be adopted to evolve a new total quality management education system (TQMES), which needs to encompass the following components:

1. *Quality Planning:* Identifying needs –this would include student's development, faculty development and development of processes.
2. *Benchmarking:* Various practices pertaining to management education need to be benchmarked.
3. *Setting Standard of Performance:* Setting Standard for every activity in the field of management education against which performance can be measured.

Quality awareness must begin at the inception of any system and should then transgress every stage so that the concept of TQM is imbibed in the whole system. Right from identifying the key players in the system to identifying the needs of the players and setting their performance standards should be done in this stage.

4. *Quality Implementation*
   - Implementation of standards.
   - Identifying the chasm between standard and actual performance level.
   - Re-formulating the plans to eliminate the causes of deviation.
   - Implementation of the reformulated plans.

This is the doing phase of the TQM system, no system can succeed until it is implemented in the right spirit and the right perspective. To make this system deliver, it is required of all the players to change the attitude, skill and knowledge.

5. *Quality Monitoring and Control*
   - Monitoring and evaluating quality system.
   - Re-designing and re-structuring plans for increasing systems efficiency.

The concept of TQM to complete a full circle requires proper monitoring and control. In this phase, the processes that do not respond to the changing needs should be over hauled and deviation, if any, should be ironed out so as to have an effective quality system.

Other Remedies

- Improving library and reading room facilities.
- Improving quality monitoring of college activities by affiliating universities.
- Giving encouragement for utilising strategies that promote self-learning in students.
- Making provision for peer feedback on class room teaching.

6
Ranking

Today ranking of B-Schools has become very common process. It is in a way assessment of strengths, weaknesses, and performance of B-Schools. Analysis of ranking of B-Schools has great importance and relevance in the present day context. It helps different stakeholders to achieve their objectives in a proper manner. The learners want to know, why they should seek admission in a particular institute. The employer wants to know about credibility, performance, and standards of the educational institute. The society wants to know how a business institute is really performing by applying different resources in a particular educational setup. The regulatory agencies intend to understand about the mode of conduct of educational programmes, evaluation system, type and standard of curriculum as well as academic standards of faculty deployed by the institution.

External ranking or benchmarking is a commonly used method for fair evaluation of performance of B-Schools. Most of the B-Schools prefer external ranking to position themselves and highlight their achievements. The significant feature of external ranking is commonly accepted, well-defined set of parameters. These parameters usually include a large number of assessment points, the spread is wide, and the coverage is exhaustive. Therefore, parametric analysis and evaluation of performance of these schools is often considered as a better method of benchmarking than any other method of evaluation.

The status and credibility of ranking agency is also a very important aspect. What kind of expertise and experience the ranking agency has, how it has collected the data, what is the methodology of assessment and its impact on overall performance assessment are some other important factors to be considered. It is necessary to understand the logic, rationale, and approach of the ranking agency while appreciating the ranking made by these institutions.

Some of the Indian B-Schools have received global and Asian recognition, these B-Schools basically concentrated on education and development of business leaders. However, if one considers performance of Indian B-Schools on important parameters like research, ranking, entry and admittance of foreign students as well as accreditation then Indian B-Schools lag significantly behind. The Asian institutes receive recognitions and accreditation from AACSB (The Association to Advance Collegiate Schools of Business). When one compares the performance of India B-Schools with B-Schools in other countries on the norm of accreditation then performance of Indian B-Schools appear very dismal.

AACSB Accreditation: How India compares with Asian Countries

Country	*Total Number of B-Schools*	*AACSB Accredited B-Schools*
Singapore	5	3
South Korea	240	14
UAE	24	4
Chinese Taipei	122	10
Thailand	108	2
China	1082	16
India	3902	2

The neglect of standards of B-Schools may result into further deterioration of quality of business education and image of India on the parameter of a country, providing good business education. In order to avoid this loss of image and opportunities of getting rightly ranked, certain steps are essential and should be taken in the best possible manner. It is urgently required that B-Schools should focus on improvement of quality, basically the quality of input and the overall standards of performance.

All the B-School Ranking award weightage to many common parameters, for example – Faculty Research, Admission, Placements, among other factors. B-School Ranking methodologies are either fact based or opinion based or a mix of the two. Ranking Methodologies attempt to arrive at the most accurate ranking order so as to give a true picture of management education in India.

'Business Today' India Best B-Schools, 2018

Leading Business magazine *Business Today's* Best B-Schools, 2018 Ranking weightages are partly fact based and partly opinion based. Here under are the top B-Schools as per ranking survey of Business Today India's Best B-Schools, 2018.

1. Indian Institute of Management, Ahmedabad
2. Indian Institute of Management, Kolkata
3. Indian Institute of Management, Bengaluru
4. XIRI, Jamshedpur Xavier School of Management
5. Management Development Institute, Gurugram (MDI), Gurugram
6. S P Jain Institute of Management and Research (SPJIMR), Mumbai
7. Indian Institute of Management, Indore
8. Indian Institute of Management, Kozhikode
9. Faculty of Management Studies (FMS), University of Delhi, Delhi

10. Indian Institute of Foreign Trade (IIFT) New Delhi
11. SVKM Narsee Monjee Institute of Management Studies (NMIMS), Mumbai
12. Institute of Management Technology (IMT), Ghaziabad
13. International Management Institute (IMI), New Delhi
14. Indian Institute of Management (IIM), Shillong
15. Great Lakes Institute of Management, Chennai
16. Indian Institute of Management, Trichy
17. Shailesh Institute of Business Management, IIT, Bombay, Mumbai
18. Symbiosis Institute of Business Management (SIBM), Pune
19. T. A. Pai Management Institute (TAPMI), Manipal
20. Department of Management Studies (IIT, Delhi), New Delhi
21. Vinod Gupta School of Management, IIT, Kharagpur
22. Xavier Institute of Management (XIMB), Bhubaneshwar
23. Jamnalal Bajaj Institute of Management Studies (JBIMS) Mumbai
24. SCMHRD Pune: Symbiosis Centre for Management and Human ResourceDevelopment
25. Indian Institute of Management (IIM), Udaipur

'Outlook' B-School Rankings, 2018

Leading current affairs magazine 'Outlook' has published its MBA Ranking, 2018 in September 2018. Rankings have awarded higher weightage to perception by awarding more than 50 per cent marks out of 1000 to Selection Process, Institute Profile, Academic Excellence and Personality Development. Here are the top 20 B-Schools as per the *Outlook* MBA College Ranking, 2018.

1. Indian Institute of Management, Kolkata
2. XLRI, Jamshedpur
3. Faculty of Management Studies (FMS), University of Delhi, Delhi
4. Indian Institute of Management, Indore
5. S P Jain Institute of Management and Research (SPJIMR), Mumbai
6. SVKM`S Narsee Monjee Institute of Management Studies (NMIMS), Mumbai
7. Management Development Institute, Gurugram (MDI),
8. Symbiosis Institute of Business Management (SIBM), Pune
9. Xavier Institute of Management, Bhubaneshwar
10. International Management Institute (IMI), New Delhi
11. Indian Institute of Management (IIM), Shillong
12. Symbiosis Centre For Management and Human Resource Development (SCMHRD), Pune:
13. Indian Institute Management (IIM), Udaipur

14. Sailesh J Mehta School of Management, IIT, Mumbai
15. T. A. Pai Management Institute (TAPMI), Manipal
16. Indian Institute of Management, Rohtak
17. Indian Institute of Foreign Trade (IIFT),New Delhi
18. Birla Institute of Technology and Science (BITS), Pilani
19. Department of Management Studies (IIT Delhi), New Delhi

MHRD-NIRF B-School Ranking, 2018

The National Institutional Ranking Framework (NIRF) is approved and released by the Ministry of Human Resource Development, Government of India. The first NIRF Ranking was released in 2016 followed by NIRF, 2017 and NIRF, 2018. As per the practice the NIRF Ranking is out in the month of April every year.

NIRF Ranking parameters broadly cover — Teaching, Learning and Resources, Research and Professional Practices, Graduation Outcomes, Outreach and Inclusivity, and Perception.

Top Institutes in NIRF MBA College Ranking, 2018

Rank	*Institute Name*	*Score*
1	Indian Institute of Management, Ahmedabad	79.18
2	Indian Institute of Management, Bengaluru	77.33
3	Indian Institute of Management,Kolkata	77.08
4	Indian Institute of Management, Lucknow	68.63
5	Indian Institute of Technology,Mumbai	66.8
6	Indian Institute of Management, Kozhikode	65.21
7	Indian Institute of Technology, Kharagpur	63.36
8	Indian Institute of Technology, Delhi	63.31
9	Indian Institute of Technology, Roorkee	62.95
10	Xavier Labour Relations Institute	62.66
11	Indian Institute of Management, Indore	60.28
12	Management Development Institute	59.59
13	Indian Institute of Management, Udaipur	59.07
14	National Institute of Industrial Engineering	57.02
15	Indian Institute of Management, Tiruchirappalli	55.85
16	Great Lakes Institute of Management	55.25
17	Indian Institute of Technology, Kanpur	53.43
18	Symbiosis Institute of Business Management	52.8
19	S. P. Jain Institute of Management and Research	52.31
20	Indian Institute of Management, Kashipur	51.2

MBA Universe.com Ranking - 2019

The 9th edition of MBA universe.com Rankings, 2018-19 are released in January 2019. This is regarded as one of India's most credible B-School Ranking and is based only on 'Objective Data' and no Perception Survey has been used. Out of more than 100 B-Schools, who participated in rankings only 80 top B-Schools have been ranked.

The ninth edition of MBAUniverse.com Rankings 2018-19, regarded as one of India's most credible B-School Ranking, was released on January 4, 2019. Conducted in guidance of Ranking Advisor Dr KRS Murthy, Former Director, IIM-Bengaluru, this Ranking is based only on 'Objective Data' and no 'Perception Survey' is used. Designed exclusively for MBA Aspirants, ranking is based on 360-degree assessment that fairly balances the three pillars of a B-School: Input (peers), Processes (academics and research) and Outcomes (placements). More 100 B-Schools participated in the ranking, while only 80 top B-Schools are ranked. First 30 of these are given below:

MBA Universe.com Ranking, 2018

Rank	*Name*
1.	Indian Institute of Management, Ahmedabad
2.	Indian Institute of Management, Lucknow
3.	XLRI Xavier School of Management, Jamshedpur
4.	S. P. Jain Institute of Management and Research (SPJIMR), Mumbai
5.	Indian Institute of Management, Indore
6.	Management Development Institute, Gurugram
7.	Faculty of Management Studies, New Delhi
8.	SVKM's Nmims, School of Business Management, Mumbai
9.	Indian Institute of Management, Tiruchirappalli
10.	Indian Institute of Management, Shillong
11.	National Institute of Industrial Engineering, Mumbai
12.	Institute of Management Technology, Ghaziabad
13.	International Management Institute, New Delhi
14.	Department of Management Studies, IIT Delhi
15.	Xavier University Bhubaneshwar (XUB)
16.	Indian Institute of Management, Rohtak
17.	Indian Institute of Management, Kashipur
18.	T A Pai Management Institute, Manipal, Karnataka
19.	Symbiosis Center For Management And Human Resource Development, Pune
20.	Goa Institute of Management, Goa
21.	Birla Institute of Management Technology, Greater Noida
22.	KJ Somaiya Institute of Management Studies and Research
23.	S.P. Mandali's Prin. L. N. Welingkar Institute of Management Development and Research, Mumbai
24.	Institute of Rural Management, Anand (IRMA)
25.	Department of Management Studies (DMS), Chennai

26.	Birla Institute of Technology and Science, Pilani
27.	Bharathidasan Institute of Management (BIM), Trichy
28.	Loyola Institute of Business Administration, Chennai
29.	Lal Bahadur Shastri Institute of Management, New Delhi
30.	Symbiosis Institute of Business Management, Bengaluru

'Times' Top 100 B-Schools

As Optimal Media Solutions Initiative, A Division of Times of India Internet Limited annually brings out Top 100 B-Schools in India. This is based on Research, Survey followed by scientifically developed analysis and ranking process. Times Top 100 B-School for 2018 are given in Appendix.

CSR-GHRDC Rankings Best B-Schools – 2018

Management education is going through changes not only in India but also elsewhere. Many questions are merging on the sustainability and dynamics taking place in this area. The CSIR GHRDC School Survey attempts to capture similarities, to showcase the transformations taking place in management education. The survey was carried out with the main purpose of evaluating the performance of management to reveal vital information for the advantage of all stakeholders concerned, i.e. aspirants, recruiters and the participating institutes and for the policy makers of our country.

The participants in the survey were voluntary. The survey formally selected 147 institutes. The data submitted by the participating institutes was rigorously verified through validation visits to the institutes followed by supplementary questions through e-mails as well as phone calls. Key factors and parameters were identified and weightages were allocated to them. Rating and ranking of all participating institutes arrived latter analysing and assessing the date against the given factors and weightage. The categorisation of institutes was done into several rating groups to help the institutes know which category they belong to. The division of the categories is defined as:

1. Ranking of Supreme B-Schools >= 80 per cent
2. Top leading B-Schools of Super Excellence >= 75 per cent to < 80 per cent
3. Top B -Schools of Super Excellence >= 70 per cent to < 75 per cent
4. Top B-Schools of Eminence >= 65 per cent to <70 per cent
5. Outstanding B-Schools of Excellence >=55 per cent to < 65 per cent
6. Top B-Schools of Excellence >= 50 per cent to < 55 per cent
7. Promising B-Schools < 50 per cent

(*See* Appendix – 4 also)

7

Master of Business Administration (MBA)

MBA (Master of Business Administration) is a terminal and a professional degree. It is an internationally accepted masters (post-graduate level) degree that:

- Imparts a strong theoretical foundation in business concepts
- Provides practical opportunities (via internships, group assignments and individual projects) to test what students learn in the class
- Builds hard-skills in the area of management and leadership
- Polishes a range of soft skills like communication, motivation and negotiation
- Opens up global opportunities for career growth
- Allows MBA students to start an independent business after graduating

Business schools in many countries offer programmes tailored to full-time, part-time, executive course work and distance-learning students, many with specialised concentrations.

Due to the economic liberalisation in India in the year 1991, the private sector unshackled which led to an increased demand for MBAs. Companies were willing to pay the top dollar to this new breed of executives, who were seen as wonder kids capable of putting family held, traditional businesses on fast track. Hence, MBA became a success mantra and management became the most sought after career for graduates. MBA symbolised status and money. Even those who managed to get into B or C grade business schools could rest assured that they had made it in life.

Unfortunately today, the degree is gradually losing its prestige. As per research, around 2,00,000 students graduated from 5,000 management institutes in the year 2016-17.While the top institutes still hold some merit in the industry, the others are hardly able to boast of quality, management education that can help their graduates secure employment and only 7 per cent turn out to be employable, says a study conducted by ASSOCHAM.

In 2016-17, more than half of MBA graduates could not get hired during campus placements. Data by All India Council of Technical Education

(AICTE) shows just 47 per cent of MBAs were placed, 4 per cent less than the previous year, and at a five year low. Data suggests that more than 220 B-Schools in top cities in India have shut down as a direct result of 45 per cent decrease in campus recruitment.

Some of the reasons for the decline of the once sought after programmes in India have been studied and well documented. However, what most analysis misses out on is a standard of evaluation and measuring the merits of a student as opposed to an institute.

Unlike the West, which has a uniform selection process of GMAT, where clear ranking and merit determines the Institute to which the student is selected. In India, we have every institute autonomously determining the admission process with no clear standard of evaluation.

Also, the qualification handed out by the various institutes ranges from a degree to a diploma, from a full-time to an online programme, all claiming to be a valid MBA degree without a measurable scale for the employer with which to evaluate. Many employers over the years have learnt the hard way that any degree holding individual is not going to take the company to new heights.

Most of these institutes are driven by commercial goals rather than educational goals and hence, quality and infrastructure are compromised rather than the fees.

However, the outdated curriculum is the main reason for the decline in the job offers to MBA degree holders in India. This has been stated before and education bodies like AICTE are working on the gap between academics and industry. The management curriculum has not been reviewed by colleges and universities as per changing corporate sector.

B-Schools are yet to see the wisdom in dovetailing their requirements and new challenges faced by the companies today.

Institutes today, also compromise on the quality of the faculty mainly due to the non-availability of good competent faculty and the cost of acquiring such faculty members. Ideally, the faculty of an MBA college must be entrepreneurs and industry leaders so that the students get to learn from their experience. Barring top institutes like IIMs. Such sessions are rarely conducted in the colleges.

Indian institutes and universities should learn from and adopt best practices from some of the best foreign universities to overcome these challenges. Possibly the biggest things that management graduates from India lack is an on the job experience.

One will never hear of poor quality graduate, coming out of colleges like Kellogs or Wharton's because they insist on work experience. It is not an entry-level degree there. The trend in India of getting an MBA first and then getting a job is a changing.

India's employability crisis is all the more serious because the majority of its population is young. Unemployed youth is one of the biggest challenges that our country faces. Private investment is down and hence, job creation is slow.

Factors that matter in choosing MBA

1. Career goals alignment
2. Batch size
3. Curriculum
4. Career support
5. Rankings
6. Placements
7. Infrastructure
8. Going ahead

The right choice has to be eventually justified by how one would spend the two years of the MBA programme. If one enhances his personality, becomes a smarter communicator (orally, in writing, in presentation skills), network with students and alumni, score good on academics, open upto business awareness and activities. Then selecting MBA programme would be justified.

Teaching Methodology

Apart from the regular lecture based teaching that most students are already familiar with MBA, pedagogy employs new methodology to ensure that the learning is maximised are case study method, group study method and group assignments.

Different Types of MBA Courses

India has lots of institutes that offer management degrees. Few among this bunch offer quality faculty and are worthy of money paid. Given that a lot of schools offer valuable education, it is becoming increasingly difficult to make the right decision about what is a top B-School. One needs information on several parameters before one can come to a conclusion about the right MBA School.

There are lots of different types of MBA courses available in India. One can select as per their working profile and area of interest.

Masters Management

- MBA in International Business
- MBA in Operations Management
- MBA in Marketing Management
- MBA in Human Resource Management
- MBA in Hospital Management

- MBA in Telecom Management
- MBA in Hospitality Management
- MBA in Retail Management
- MBA in Entrepreneurship and Leadership
- MBA in Finance and Accounting
- MBA in Insurance Management
- MBA in Marketing and Sales
- MBA in Operations and Production Management
- MBA in Logistics and Supply Chain Management
- MBA in General Management
- MBA in E-Business Management
- MBA in Hospital Administration
- MBA in Entrepreneurship
- Master of Business Administration
- MBA in Banking Management
- MBA in Business Analytics and Intelligence
- MBA in Business Leadership
- MBA in E-Commerce Marketing and Management
- MBA in Financial Planning and Analysis
- MBA in Foreign Trade and Global Business Management
- MBA in International Marketing
- MBA in Investment Banking and Wealth Management
- MBA in Project Leadership and Management
- MBA in Risk Management
- MBA in Strategic Management
- Master in Risk Management
- Master in Human Resources and Organisation
- Master in the Science of Public Administration
- Master in International Business Administration
- MBA in Innovation Management
- MBA in Investment Management
- MBA in Pharma Management
- MBA in Strategic Finance
- MBA in Finance Management
- MBA in Management
- Master of Public Administration
- MBA in Business Analytics
- MBA in Rural Management
- MBA in Oil and Gas
- MBA in Power Management
- MBA in Petroleum and Natural Gas Management
- MBA in Agricultural Management

Popular Courses/ Specialisations

Competition Success Review (November, 2018) describes in detail the popular specialisations or courses.

There are a number of specialisations in the MBA, some of which have universal demand. While an MBA or a PGDM is itself sufficient to equip one with the technical skills to make a mark in the corporate world, a specialisation in the area of one's choice not only gives one satisfaction but also infuses lifelong enthusiasm to excel professionally. An MBA or a PGDM can be pursued at any age and thus, add to one's quality of achievement in a decent manner. If an individual wants to acquire managerial skills, he/she should do an MBA or PGDM and for this she/she should be a simple graduate in any stream or a technical degree holder. Usually, people from all spheres try to enhance their accomplishments with an MBA or a PGDM. They more often select one specialisation from the list on offer in the institution they are admitted into. The list contains both traditional and unconventional choices. While emerging specialisations are umpteen, the traditional ones, such as – Financial Management, Marketing Management, Human Resource Management and Operations Management have their own charm. These areas have enjoyed a lot of popularity due to their utility and importance in running a business on the whole.

Financial Management

Nature of Financial Management

Financial Management is one of the important areas of education, which is pursued across the world. Financial management is a long-term decision-making process, which involves a lot of planning, allocation of funds, discipline etc. These days, people take up various specialisation courses of financial management. Many people have chosen financial management as their profession.

- The nature of financial management is never a separate entity. Even as an operational manger or functional manager, one has to take the responsibility of financial management.
- Financial is a component of economic activities. A financial manager controls the finance and implements the plans. For any company, the financial manger plays a crucial role. Many times, the lack of skills or wrong decisions can lead to heavy loses to an organisation.
- Nature of financial management is multi-disciplinary. Financial management depends upon various other factors like accounting, banking, inflation economy etc. for the better utilisation of finances.
- Approach of financial management is not limited to business functions but it is the backbone of commerce and industry.

Goals of Financial Management

Financial management can be called a good guide for allotment of future resources of an organisation. It is generally concerned with procurement, allocation and control of financial resources of a concern. The objectives can be:

- To ascertain regular and adequate supply of funds to the concern.
- To ensure adequate returns to the stakeholders, which depend upon the earning capacity, market price of the share, expectations of the stakcholders.
- To ensure optimum funds utilisation. Once the funds are procured, they should be utilised in the best possible way at the minimum cost.
- To ensure safety on investment i.e. funds should be invested in safe ventures so that adequate rate of return can be achieved.
- To plan a sound capital structure, there should be sound and fair composition of capital so that a balance is maintained between debt and equity capital.

Functions of Financial Management

The main functions of financial management system are:

1. Executive functions
2. Routine functions

The executive functions of financial management are:

1. Raising the funds required
2. Assessing total capital requirement
3. Deciding the capital requirement
4. Deciding the capital structure
5. Estimating the cost of capital
6. Management of fixed capital
7. Management of working capital
8. Allotment of excess profit
9. Planning tax
10. Performance evaluation

Routine functions of financial management are:

1. Maintain various books of accounts of the companies
2. Administration of cash receipts and payments
3. Maintain cash balances of the company
4. Preserving securities, insurance policies and other valuable papers
5. Preparing final accounts
6. Interacting with banks
7. Keeping records and reporting
8. Assisting a finance executive in the performance of his/her roles.

Marketing Management

The increasing competition has necessitated the need for competitive positioning and excellent marketing skills including tje ability to differentiate the product and creating a niche for a company in order to sustain long-term profitability for its products or services. Marketing management is the art and service of setting target markets and getting, keeping and growing customer base through creating, delivering and communicating superior customer value. Marketing management is an organisational discipline, which focuses on the practical application of marketing orientation and on the management of a firm's marketing resources and activities.

It is chiefly concerned with the chalking out of a definite programme, after careful analysis and forecasting of the market situations and the ultimate execution of these plans to achieve the objectives of the organisation.

MBA in marketing offers a very dynamic and competitive career to its aspirants. It helps one to understand consumer behaviour, market behaviour, aspects of advertising, and many other crucial skills that surround the marketing activities of any product/service.MBA in Marketing can increase the chances of receiving a promotion. The variety of business, leadership skills and knowledge attained through an MBA programme help graduates qualify for management and executive positions. With enough relevant professional experience, MBA marketing graduates may advance to positions as Marketing Managers or Directors, Marketing and Business Development Managers and Brand Managers.

Significance of Marketing Management

- Marketing is helpful in the development of an economy. It is the force that sets the economy revolving. The marketing organisations, more scientifically organised, make the economy strong and stable. The lesser the stress on the marketing function, the weaker will be the economy.
- Marketing is very helpful in transfer, exchange and movement of goods. Goods and services are made available to customers through various intermediaries viz., wholesalers, retailers etc .It is helpful to booth producers and consumers.
- Marketing gives employment to many people. It is estimated that about 40 per cent of the total population is directly or indirectly dependent upon marketing. In the modern era of large scale production and industrialisation, role of marketing has widened.
- Marketing is source of income and revenue. The performance of marketing function is all important because it is the only way through which the concern can generate revenue or income and bring in profits.

- Marketing acts as a basis for making decisions. A businessman is confronted with many problems in the form of what, how, when, how much and for whom to produce? In the past, the problems were less on account of local marketers. There was a direct link between producer and consumer but in the modern times, marketing has become a very complex and tedious task. Marketing has emerged as a new specialised activity along with production. As a result, producers are depending largely on the mechanism of marketing, to decide what to produce and sell.

Human Resource Management

Human refers to the skilled workforce in the organisation; Resource refers to limited availability or scarce; and Management refers to maximise or proper utilisation and make best use of limited and scarce resources. Thus, Human Resource Management is the process of proper and maximum utilisation of available limited skilled workforce. Human resource management (HRM) is the strategic approach to the effective management of organisation workers so that they help the business gain a competitive advantage. It involves recruitment and selection of employees, providing compensation and benefits, motivating, maintaining proper relations with employees and with trade unions, maintaining employees' safety, welfarc and health measures in compliance with labour laws of the land.

Components of Human Resources

The purpose of human resource is to ensure that the organisation is able to achieve success through people. HR professionals manage the human capital of an organisation and focus on implementing policies and processes. They can specialise in recruiting, training, employee relations or benefits. Human resource management is a process, which involves four basic components – acquisition, development, motivation and maintenance of human resources. These basic elements are the key steps for achieving organisational goals.

Goals of Human Resource Management

Human Resource Management is useful not only for an organisation, but also for the employees working therein. Moreover, the society at large also finds it useful. The objectives of HRM are as under:

Organisational Objective: To recognise that HRM exists to contribute to organisational effectiveness.HRM is not an end in itself; it is only a means to assist to organisation with its primary objectives. In simple words, the department exists to serve the rest of the organisation.

Functional Objective: To maintain the department's contribution at the level appropriate to the needs of the organisation. Resources are wasted, when HRM is more or less sophisticated than the organisation demands. A department's level of service must be appropriate for the organisation it serves.

Personal Objective: To assist employees in achieving their personal goals, so far as these goals enhance the individual's contribution to the organisation. Personal objectives of employees must be met, if workers are to be maintained and retained.

Operations Management

Operations Management is an area of management concerned with planning, designing, organising and controlling the process of production and re-designing business operations in the context of production of goods or services. It is delivery focused, and ensures that an organisation successfully and efficiently turns inputs into outputs. The inputs themselves could represent anything from materials, equipment and technology to human resources such as staff or workers. This arm of the business forum is responsible for ascertaining that the company produces a product efficiently and ultimately helps in the profitability of the company while also making sure that the customers are happy with their final product .Operations Management is about how organisations produce or deliver the goods and services that provide the reason for their existence. Operations can be seen as one of the many functions (e.g. marketing, finance, personnel) within the organisation. The operations function can be described as that part of organisation which is devoted to the production or delivery of goods and services. This means that all organisations undertake operations activities because every organisation undertakes operations activities because every organisation produces goods and/or services. Operations Management involves the supervision and coordination of operations related to the production of goods. If you have strong problem solving and leadership skills, this field of business may be right for you. Most Master's degree programmes in Operations Management are designed with the working professional in mind. These programmes cover various methods and tools that can be used to effectively govern people, projects and processes. Studies in operations management afford a wide range of career options to the graduates depending on the area of specialisation.

MBA in operations management helps you in dealing with production management or shop floor management related functions. You learn how to maintain process flows, develop vendor and inter-departmental relationships. MBA in operations management covers various methods and tools that can be used to effectively manage a range of work settings for various organisations. Along with the essential concepts of operations management, students can learn about specialised areas, such as Business management, human resource management or industrial management through elective courses. Applicants need to provide transcripts from every university and college attended, when applying for a programme. Core curriculum within a Master's degree programme for operations management addresses:

- Human behaviour
- Quality management
- Cost analysis
- Ethics in leadership
- Project planning
- Decision making principles

The following are the main objectives of operations management:

- Producing the right kind of goods and services that satisfy customers' needs (effectiveness objective)
- Maximising output of goods and services with minimum resource inputs (efficiency objective)
- Ensuring that goods and services produced conform to pre-set quality specifications (quality objective)
- Minimising throughput-time – the time that elapses in the conversion process – by reducing delays, waiting time and idle time (lead time objective)
- Maximising the utilisation of manpower, machines etc. (Capacity utilisation objective)
- Minimising the cost of producing goods or rendering a service (cost objective)

Responsibilities of Operations Management

Operations management is the business function that is responsible for planning, organising, coordinating and controlling the resources needed to produce a company's products and services. Operations management handles various strategic issues including determining the size of manufacturing plants and project management methods and implementing the structure of information technology networks. Other operational issues include the management of inventory levels including work in process levels and raw materials acquisition, quality control; materials handling; and maintenance policies. Operations management entails studying the use of raw materials and ensuring that minimal occurs .Managers utilise numerous formulas, such as the economic order quality formula to determine when and how much inventory to hold in hand.

Career Prospects in Operations Management

Operations management has emerged as a lucrative career option among the youth in India and abroad. It offers wide range of career opportunities in the field of construction, consulting firms, financial institutions, hospitality, information technology, insurance, manufacturing, retail, transportation and logistics. One can work as customer service support, distribution and supply chain manger, forecasting, inventory planner and control. Operations planner, scheduling and control, purchasing and materials manager, project manager, process and methods planner, plant engineering manager, quality manager, operations process consulting personnel, traffic manager, warehouse manager and distributors etc. Some of the most common areas of work include supply chain management, logistics planning, inventory control management or business consultation.

Distance MBA

Distance MBA is now duly approved course by University Grants Commission (UGC). The UGC (Online Courses) Regulations, 2018, has announced on May 24, 2018 that higher educational institutions can offer the distance learning online degree, diploma and certificate courses at par with their regular classroom programmes.

Institutions, which have been offering such courses, duly approved by the statutory authority, at the undergraduate level as regular classroom programmes, or as open and distance learning programmes, and where at least one batch has graduated, are eligible to offer distance learning programmes. Such online Distance learning programmes require a minimum National Assessment and Accreditation Council (NAAC) score of 3.26 on the 4-point scale.

If you are looking for Distance MBA courses, there are hundreds of MBA colleges offering Distance MBA in India. But, there are only very few that offer good value for your time and effort. This article by MBAUniverse.com experts will help you decide which Distance MBA Programme to select.

What is Distance MBA?

Distance MBA course is a flexible and affordable Government recognised MBA programme which does not require you to attend regular daily classes. So, if you are unable to pursue full time MBA for lack of time or due to high cost, Distance MBA Education is a good option. The Top Distance MBA colleges in India offer offline Correspondence MBA, Online MBA or a combination of two in Distance Learning mode. Distance education, including Distance MBA, is controlled by University Grants Commission (UGC), which is working to improve the quality and better governance in this sector.

Types of Distance MBA Colleges

Ministry of HRD, Government of India, has recognised four types of institutions to offer Distance Education and Distance MBA in India:

1. Distance MBA offered by National Open University or IGNOU
2. Distance MBA offered by State Open Universities
3. Distance Education Institutions (DEIs) at Institutions of National Importance
   - Central Universities
   - State Universities
   - Deemed to be Universities
   - State Private Universities
4. Distance MBA offered by DEIs at stand-alone Institutions
   - Professional Associations
   - Government Institutions
   - Private Institutions

Best Distance MBA Colleges in India

Some of the best Distance MBA Colleges in India are:

- NMIMS Global Access School for Continuing Education
- Symbiosis Centre for Distance Learning (SCDL)
- IMT-Centre for Distance Learning (IMT-CDL) Ghaziabad
- Indira Gandhi National Open University (IGNOU)
- Sikkim Manipal University- Distance Education, Sikkim

Key Benefits of Distance MBA

If you are still having doubts, Distance MBA Programmes offers a lot of benefits and advantages for students and working professionals. Key benefits are:

1. *Effective time management*: Distance MBA offers flexibility of time and pace over regular MBA. It is well suited for people, who due to time, money or other constraints cannot afford to do full time MBA.
2. *Power of education technology, direct to your home*: Distance MBA education has greatly benefited from the rise of communication and education technology. Even premier Universities and B-Schools such as MIT and Harvard Business School use education technology to deliver programmes across the world. Further, MOOCs and platforms such as Coursera, Edex and Udacity have removed the stigma associated with distance education.
3. *Cost effective option:* One of the biggest advantages of the Distance MBA programmes is its low fee structure. While a regular MBA can cost you anywhere in between 5-15 Lakhs, good Distance MBA Programmes fee ranges from Rs 75,000 to Rs 1.5 lakhs.
4. *Industry relevant curriculum*: Best Distance MBA institutes like NMIMS University, Symbiosis Center for Distance Learning and IMT CDL are well aware of changing business environment and

hence offer an updated and industry relevant curriculum to the students.

5. *Recognised by Regulatory Bodies:* Distance MBA offered by recognised MBA colleges are approved by UGC's Distance Education Bureau (DEB). You can check about the status of approval of any distance MBA programme by visiting DEB website.

Distance MBA Eligibility Criteria

The eligibility for Distance MBA varies according to the institute and duration of the programme. However, the common 2 year Distance MBA Eligibility Criteria are:

- Bachelor's degree/ graduation from a recognised University
- A valid score in any of MBA entrance exam like State Level MBA/ MMS-CET/ MAT/] CMAT/ CAT/ ATMA/ XAT or equivalent management entrance test.
- Some colleges conduct their own entrance test if you don't have any other test score
- Work Experience is preferred, but it is not an essential requirement

Top Distance MBA Colleges in India

There are hundreds of MBA colleges offering Distance MBA in India. But, there are only very few top distance leading management colleges that offer good value. Best Distance MBA colleges have a few common features: Recognition by UGC, good Brand name, Update curriculum and affordable fee.

Careers

An MBA prepares individuals for many types of careers. According to a survey by the Graduate Management Admissions Council, 64 per cent of the year 2012 MBA graduates used their MBA to change careers. Some of the more common jobs, an MBA prepares one for include:

- Business analyst or strategist
- Business development analyst, associate or manager
- Director of a department)
- Entrepreneur/founder
- Financial analyst
- Management consultant
- Marketing associate, analyst or manager
- Portfolio manager
- Project product or programme manager
- Operations analyst, associate or manager

Un-met Needs of MBA Programme

Despite phenomenal expansion of Management Education, the B-School of the country need to focus on to eight un-met needs of MBA programme as espoused by Datar, Garvin and Cullen (2010) in the following framework so that they remain relevant in the times to come.

1. *Gaining a global perspective*: Identifying, analysing and practicing how best to manage when faced with economic, institutional and cultural differences across the countries.
2. *Developing leadership skills:* Understanding the responsibilities of leadership, developing alternative approaches to inspiring, influencing and guiding others; learning such skills as conducting a performance review and giving critical feedback; and recognising the impact of one's actions and behaviours on others.
3. *Honing integration skills*: Thinking about issues from diverse, shifting angles to frame problems holistically; learning to make decisions based on multiples, often conflicting, functional perspectives; and building judgment and intuition into messy, unstructured situations.
4. *Recognising organisational realities and implementing effectively*: Influencing others and getting things done in the context of hidden agenda, unwritten rules, political coalitions, and competing points of views.
5. *Acting creatively and innovatively:* Finding and framing problems; collecting, synthesising and distilling large volumes of ambiguous data: engaging in generative and lateral thinking; and constantly experimenting and learning.
6. *Thinking critically and communicating clearly*: Developing and articulating logical, coherent, and persuasive arguments; marshalling supportive evidences; and distinguishing facts from opinion.
7. *Understanding the role, responsibilities and purpose of business:* Balancing financial and non-financial objectives while simultaneously juggling the demands of diverse constituencies such as shareholder, employees, customer, regulators and society.
8. *Understanding the limits of models and markets:* Asking tough questions about risk by questioning underlying assumptions and emerging patterns; seeking to understand what might go wrong; learning about the sources of errors that lead to flawed decision-making and the organisational safeguards that reduce their occurrence; and understanding the tension between regulatory activities aimed at preventing social harm and market based incentives designed to encourage innovation and efficiency.

MBA Value Comes Down

Is it true that the value of MBA has come down and it is no longer a popular programme? No. It is not true. A recent alumni perspectives survey carried out by the Graduate Management Admission Council of MBA alumni from about 15000 B-Schools around the globe reveals that the alumni not only highly value their MBA degree but also admit that they have reaped multiple benefits from completing their programme. 93 per cent of them said that the MBA degree was personally rewarding and they are highly likely to recommend it to others. In specific terms they say that MBA prepared them for their chosen career, increased their earning power, quick career advancement, job satisfaction and developed their professional network.

MBA degree has already established its credibility with business and industry. Despite the ups and downs in the economy there has been a continued and widespread acceptance of MBAs by the employers.

It is a versatile degree which opens the door to several career paths. The knowledge and skills acquired in the programme can be applied to all areas of business and across several industries. It provides scope for career change and social mobility. It also helps in starting one's own enterprise right from the beginning.

For hard working and highly motivated MBAs, in addition to their personal development, it has also been a stepping stone for lucrative jobs. In a recent survey conducted by AMBA (Association of MBAs), it was found that "nearly 58 per cent of the MBA graduates have moved into senior management or CEO roles". Today, it is Indian MBAs who run some of the world's biggest organisations from Google to Microsoft, Pepsi to Coca-Cola, Cognizant to Net App, Adobe to MasterCard.

While the Indian economy is getting diversified, the demand for MBAs, is likely to increase in a broad spectrum of industries in the coming years. Employers are in search of talented individuals who have leadership qualities, communication skills, strategic thinking and analytical mind which are in fact the foundation of a good MBA programme.

Attributes Lacking in MBA Students

HR managers from 10 companies in Hyderabad were interacted to understand the present quality of management graduates. The Managers perceived that the following attributes were lacking in students:

1. Technical skills
2. Passion/interest in career development
3. Analytical skills
4. Communication skills
5. Awareness about industry

6. Career decision making skills
7. Flexible/adaptable skills
8. Problem solving skills
9. Awareness about career options
10. Application of knowledge
11. Goal setting
12. Values and ethics
13. Business knowledge
14. Learning skills
15. Enthusiasm

Skills Lacking in MBA Students

Academicians perceived that the following skills were lacking in the students:

1. Communication skills
2. Technical/domain skills
3. Language skills
4. Learning aptitude
5. Ethics
6. Leadership skills
7. Team building skills
8. Time management skills
9. Etiquette
10. Decision making skills
11. Critical thinking skills
12. Lateral thinking skills

Top 10 Qualities of a Great MBA Student

Today, an MBA is one of the most sought after graduate degrees and is the most popular online degree programme. But though it is increasing in popularity, it is still a rigorous and challenging as ever. To succeed in a competitive MBA programme an MBA candidate should have certain characteristics and here are the 10 qualities of a great MBA student:

1. *Commitment and Focus*: An MBA programme isn't a cakewalk, and the most successful students are the ones who are absolutely committed to the programme and to their own career goals. You should have a clear idea of why you want an MBA and what you want it do for your career. Keeping a strong focus on your goals will help you maximize your programme's offerings and give you the most bangs for your buck throughout the programme.
2. *Communication Skills:* Any effective business leader has to have great communication skills, and it certainly helps, if those communication

skills are honed before starting B-School! Great written communication skills, especially, will be imperative in an online MBA programme since you'll likely be limited to using email and other online methods of communication to reach your professors and classmates.

3. *Creativity*: Some of today's top businesses are those who think "outside the box" and develop ingenious solutions to common problems. An MBA candidate should be very creative and be able to come up with innovative and realistic ideas for their organisation.
4. *Decision Making Skills:* A key aspect of leadership and management is being able to make effective decisions and think quickly on your feet this is something that may good MBA candidate will need to have during school to successfully complete assignments and participate in activities.
5. *Discipline*: A great online MBA candidate should be very self-disciplined. Not only does an MBA involve intensive course-work, but also the freedom of an online format makes it easier to become distracted worth other projects. To get a good grasp of the material and to make sure the work is being completed, you'll need to have great time management skills and be able to keep yourself in check.
6. *Entrepreneurship*: The most successfully MBA students and business leaders have a strong sense of entrepreneurship. They are interested in being innovative and have a strong commitment to success. They are driven and extremely motivated.
7. *Ethics*: The most successful business leaders are those who practice with sound ethics in mind, and the ethics are key to getting through business school, as well,. In addition to understanding why good business decisions are made on the basis of ethical codes, it's important to work within your schools and your own ethical guidelines.
8. *Leadership*: An MBA is a degree designed for those interested in leadership roles in their organisations, so the best candidates for an MBA will have strong leadership skills as well as an interest in increasing such skills.
9. *Logical Analysis*: Many MBA courses involve logical thought processes, and thus, the most successful students have a strong sense of logical analysis. They are able to think through complex situations quickly and clearly to develop smart solutions and ideas.
10. *Team Oriented*: Just as a successful business is the work of all its employees, so is the work of an MBA candidate, MBA students will often be called upon to work in teams on various projects and great students will be able to handle the group work without a problem. An online MBA student, especially, should feel comfortable working with others through email and chat programmes or even through the occasional face-to-face meeting.

List of Important Skills Valued by MBA Recruiters

Priority	*Counselling*	*Finance/ Accounting*	*Technology*	*Manufacturing*
1	Fit with company culture	Fit with company culture	Ability to make an impact	Ability to make an impact
2	Ability to work in and build strong teams	Ability to work in and build strong teams	Fit with company culture	Leadership potential
3	Ability to make an impact	Ability to make an impact	Ability to work in and build strong teams	Fit with company culture
4	Adaptability	Leadership potential	Leadership potential	Ability to work in and build strong teams
5	Strong business ethics	Adaptability	Ability to use data to tell a story	Ability to use data to tell a story

Types of MBA

1. *Two year (Full Time) MBA*: This is the main programme offered by almost all colleges in the country. The colleges, which are autonomous like the IIM's offer a post-graduate diploma in management (PGDM) or Post-graduate Programme in Management (PGPM). According to AICTE only registered universities can provide an MBA degree. The difference between the diploma and degree is not much while an MBA degree focuses on the theoretical aspects of business, a diploma is more industry oriented with a focus on case-studies.
2. *Accelerated MBA*: This is like crash course in MBA with tightly packed classes and an aim to finish the full time MBA as soon as possible.
3. *Part-time MBA*: This programme is specially designed for the working professionals. The duration of this programme is longer, about 3 years, as the classes are held on weekdays after working hours or over the weekend. This is a more flexible kind of a programme.
4. *Executive MBA*: This programme is devised specifically for working professionals, who generally have more than two years of work experience. It is very similar to the generally have than two years of work experience. It is very similar to the general MBA programme but is designed to provide education to managers, executives, entrepreneurs, and other business leaders, executive MBA is part-time. Apart from this a number of colleges offer the one year executive MBA programme based

on GMAT scores. They include ISB, IIMB, EPGP, IIMA PGPX, IIMC, PGPEX and XLRI GMP to name a few.

After the completion of this programme one can continue to work at their current position or look at better avenues. The ability to accept different kinds of responsibilities increases making the individual an important asset for the smooth functioning of the company.

5. *Distance Learning MBA*: These programmes are attained through non-interactive broadcast video, correspondence courses by postal mail or email, live teleconference courses by postal mail or email, live teleconference or video conference, pre-recorded video, and offline or online computer courses. A number of universities like Symbiosis, IGNOU, Annamalai, etc., are well known for their distance learning programmes.
6. *Dual MBA*: This is where a normal MBA degree is combined with another, like MS or MA.
7. Online MBA: Since the dawn of smart phone, 3G tablets, and broad-band, students, who are not able to enroll in a normal course can obtain the education of their choice online. Management related lectures and case-studies are uploaded, which can be readily accessed. There is no requirement of attending classes and assignments and exams are also conducted online.

Making Right Career Decision

Before opting for MBA Courses, we present some facts to assist you in making the right career decision.

- Nearly 6,000 educational institutes MBA studies are in India. These include government run private and foreign universities.
- Educational institutes in India offer MBA courses of two to four year duration.
- You can do an MBA by home studies, online or distance education or conventional classroom courses from most of these universities.
- An MBA course can cost anything between Rs. 1,50,000 to Rs. 1 million, depending upon the educational institute.
- MBA courses from across India enroll the 20 plus top ranking business schools of India witness the greatest demand from students.
- An estimated 5,00,000 students across India enroll for MBA courses of all types every year.
- About 3,50,000 students graduate as MBAs from various universities every year.

Employment for MBAs

Considering the above facts, it is evident that India churns out the highest number of MBA degree holders annually.

Unfortunately, a report compiled by the Associated Chambers of Commerce and Industry of India (ASSOCHAM)) in 2017 reveals some rather disappointing facts.

Highlights of this report include:

- Less than 10 per cent of MBA holders in India get employment.
- Among those MBAs who find work, the average salary is just about Rs.10, 000 per month.
- Quality of training for MBA curses in India, especially at private universities and online MBA courses is rather poor. Hence, graduates are generally ill-qualified for jobs traditionally held by MBA degree holders.
- Employment opportunities are bright only for MBA degree holders, who graduate from prestigious business schools or state run universities of India.

According to a report complied early 2017 by the All India Council for Technical Education, the country will witness a huge demand for MBA in coming years.

This demand will be filled by the Make in India, Skills India and opening up of more sectors in this country and Foreign Direct Investment and Foreign Institutional Investment.

The report encouragingly states, between 35,000 and 40,000 MBA graduates will be needed at junior and middle level managerial positions for the Indian private and public sectors every year.

Regardless, to embark on a successful career, you will have to enroll for an MBA course in some specialised field, for different MBA courses offered by top-notch business schools and state run universities.

Understandably, selecting the best MBA course in India can prove cumbersome.

However, with adequate research, you can find a top-notch business school which offers globally acceptable qualifications. Remember about MBA courses are relatively expensive.

Hence, completing a course without acquiring proper and practical skills will only waste your precious time, effort and money.

Getting into IIMs, IITs, Symbiosis, NMIMS, SPJIMR and other reputed B-Schools requires extra effort.

However, such additional efforts are worthwhile while considering your prospects in any industry.

MBA Transforms Personality and Outlook

MBA is a fast track real world simulation in 2 years. It is designed in such a way that a student faces a wide range of situations to which he needs to respond to in a short time. This leads to the disadvantage of creative thinking in students. Vidha Gaur explains how MBA helps shape the personality for a successful career. How this in her own words:

Critical Thinking: In the age of the internet, we are surrounded by a plethora of information. What we learn at MBA is how to 'filter the information' from all, 'obtain insights' from that and 'apply those insights by suggesting solutions to complex problems'.

Time Management: Our demanding life styles demand that we prioritise the important things and allocate the time accordingly. MBAs rigorous curriculum demands the same.

Communication Skills: MBA with the help of presentations and diversity that it brings to class helps students to level up the confidence. They not only become more fluent in verbal skills but also learn how to convey a message in a meaningful manner by understanding the receiver.

Decision- making and Right Attitude: "Your life is a garland of choices and decisions woven by a thread, and that thread is you." Among the diverse crowd and rigorous curriculum of MBA students learn to recognise what's right for them and along with some courage, a student can emerge as a strong personality with clarity and refined actions.

Networking: Not only you meet people from diverse geographies and backgrounds but also build a strong network of friends and seniors working in top companies giving you an edge in the competitive world.

Leadership Skills: Students during first year study all subjects, thus building a 360 degree perspective. They also learn to identify their own strengths and weaknesses and leverage their colleagues' strengths while working in teams. This helps them to evolve as a well-rounded personality with the ability to lead and work in top management positions.

Ensuring Quality

P K Das in 2013, in *Asian Journal of Management Research* suggested the following actions to ensure quality in MBA:

Training and research in MBA programme should commensurate with the requirements for ensuring quality. Student enrolment has become lopsided with rapid expansion of business programmes. With entry of private players in the field of technical education has made it more acute;

- Accrediting bodies from across the world may accredit the programme of a B-Schools but those accrediting bodies, first of all, must be recognised by the AICTE and the UGC;
- Foreign players and big business may come to the education field, but they must ensure that their syllabi are at least as good or better than those approved by the AICTE and the UGC;

- The fee structure may be regulated so that it would not be unfavourable to the first generation learners, socially disadvantaged groups; women and other backward sections of the society;
- Selection of students may be done through one or two all India level tests. Those tests must contain tests of aptitude for management education. Apart from scoring 50 per cent marks in each of the examinations from 10th to the bachelor degree level, a student must score at least 50 per cent marks in the tests to be eligible for getting admission;
- The number of MBA programmes must be made limited. A general MBA with four or five specialisation types such as Marketing, Finance, Human Resources and Operations may be considered. A project on a particular industry may make a student eligible for a job in that industry;
- Student attendance must be made compulsory and centralised. Electronic devices may be used for both faculty and students to ensure their presence in the classes;
- In order to maintain parity amongst the passing our students, an all India test of competence may be made compulsory to rank the students for being eligible for various jobs in the government as well as private sector units;
- MBA may be treated as a professional degree on par with charted accountants, cost accountants, doctors, lawyers and company secretaries.
- These apart, a standard salary structure in the line of minimum wage may be implemented for MBA. This would not only ensure good inputs for MBA education but also would help this stream of trained manpower flourish in the global market.

8

MBA Entrance Tests

There are a number of National Level MBA Entrance Tests today. Various national level MBA entrance test to get into the top B-Schools in India are indicated below:

- CAT (Common Admission Test, CAT): The Common Admission Test is conducted by IIMs as a qualification for admission to various management programmes of IIMs, IITs and IISc for their MBA programmes.
- MAT: The AIMA use this test, Management Aptitude Test, for granting admission to its MBA and equivalent courses. MAT is a National Entrance Test.
- XAT- Xavier Aptitude Test is conducted by XLRI on behalf of the Xavier Association of Management Institutes (XAMI). XAT scores will be used by XLRI Jamshedpur and other Xavier Associate Management Institutes and over 120 B-Schools across the country for admission.
- IGNOU OPENMAT is conducted by the Indira Gandhi National Open University (IGNOU) for admission to their management programmes.
- ATMA: AIMS, Hyderabad, conducts the AIMS ATMA Entrance Test for Management courses for admissions in its participating institutes across India for MBA admissions.
- SNAP- Symbiosis National Aptitude Test is a common written test for the admission to all the PG Institutes of Symbiosis International (Deemed) University which runs management programmes.
- IBSAT: The ICFAI Business School Aptitude Test is an online aptitude test conducted by ICFAI for admission to the MBA / Ph.D programmes of IBS Hyderabad.
- CMAT: The Common Management Admission Test is a national-level admission test for aiding institutions to select suitable students for admission in all management programmes approved by AICTE.
- NMIMS NMAT: Narsee Monjee Institute of Management Studies School of Business Management conduct the paper for admission to its vast MBA programmes, both general management and specialised areas.

- GMAT: GMAT stands for "Graduate Management Admissions Test". The GMAT is managed by the Graduate Management Admissions Council (GMAC). Admissions teams evaluating applicants to graduate programmes in management use GMAT scores as a key supplemental factor in considering an applicant's qualifications along with other factors such as undergraduate performance and work experience.
- CUSAT: Cochin University of Science and Technology (CUSAT) conducts entrance exam for admission to various academic programmes of the University for the academic year 2018-19. All admissions are on the basis of online Common Admission Test (CAT) or online Lateral Entry Test (LET) or Departmental Admission Test (DAT) conducted by the University Admission to MBA Programme is based on C-MAT (AICTE) / MAT (AIMA) / CAT (IIM) score, GD and Interview and for M.Tech GATE score.
- IIFT: The Indian Institute of Foreign Trade (IIFT) invites applications for Master of Business Administration (MBA - International Business) Degree Programme at New Delhi, Kolkata and Kakinada (Andhra Pradesh) Campuses, academic year 2018-20.
- IPUCET: Guru Gobind Singh Indraprastha University, Delhi has announced the dates for Common Entrance Test (IPU CET, 2018), the result of which will be considered for admission to programmes of its centers for the academic year 2018-19.
- CUCET: It is a combined entrance test, organised for providing admission into various UG, PG and other courses offered by the central universities across the country.
- BVPB-MAT: Bharati Vidyapeeth Deemed University conducts BVP B-MAT for admission to MBA Programme.
- SAAT- SAAT 2018 is the Common Entrance Exam for Siksha 'O' Anusandhan University admission to UG and PG courses.
- KIITEE MBA: This is the All India Entrance Examination conducted by (Kalinga Institute of Industrial Technology) (KIIT University), Bhubaneswar for admission into following courses of the University. The notification for KIIT University Entrance Exam KIITEE 2018 has been announced.
- LPA NEST: The Lovely Professional University conducts the entrance test for various Undergraduate, Post-graduate and Degree Programmes, such as B.Tech, MBA, BHMCT etc.
- PTU MBA: Punjab Technical University PTU MBA Entrance Test
- MICAT: Mudra Institute of Communications (MIC), Ahmedabad invites applications for admissions to Post Graduate Diploma in Management – Communications.

- NIMIMS NPAT: NPAT is the official entrance test for admissions to Undergraduate Degree and Integrated Degree Programmes being offered by constituent schools of SVKM's Narsee Monjee Institute of Management Studies at Mumbai, Shirpur, Bengaluru, Indore and Navi Mumbai Campuses.
- IMUCET: Indian Maritime University organises a Common Entrance Test.

Some details of the tests are given below, but for any change details may be checked from the concerned institute.

1. Common Admission Test (CAT)

The biggest and most popular entrance examination of India, Common Admission Test or CAT is conducted by the Indian Institute of Management (IIM). CAT scores are used for admission by 20 IIMs and various other management institutes across the country. More than two lakh students appear for the exam each year.

CAT started in 1950 and graduated to being an online-entrance test in 2009. The CAT question paper consists of 100 questions (MCQs) to be solved in 180 minutes. Registration for CAT begins in August-September and the exam is held in November-December.

2. Common Management Admission Test (CMAT)

The second largest management entrance examination of the country, Common Management Admission Test or CMAT is taken by roughly 1.5 lakh candidates. Conducted by the National Testing Agency, CMAT is a popular option among MBA aspirants after CAT. The first CMAT exam took place in 2012. However, it has fast become one of the most popular exams of the country. The exam is accepted by more than 500 MBA institutes across the country. The CMAT exam is held in January every year.

CMAT is a computer-based exam (held for 180 minutes) and tests the candidate's aptitude in four main sections:

- Quantitative technique
- Logical reasoning
- Language comprehension
- General Awareness

3. Xavier Aptitude Test (XAT)

Another top management entrance, XAT is a computer based management aptitude test which is conducted by XLRI on behalf of the Xavier Association of Management Institutes. XAT is taken by approximately One Lakh candidates annually.

Traditionally, XAT is held on the first Sunday of the year (January). XAT scores are accepted by more than 100 management institutes.

XAT exam tests the candidate on four fronts:

- Quantitative Ability
- English Language and Logical Reasoning
- Decision Making
- GK and Essay

However, easy section is used only after candidates have been shortlisted for XLRI courses. Test duration is 170 minutes.

4. Symbiosis National Aptitude Test (SNAP)

Conducted by Symbiosis International University, Symbiosis National Aptitude Test or SNAP is also a national-level management entrance examination. SNAP scores are primarily used for admission to 15 institutes under Symbiosis International University. However, many other MBA colleges use SNAP scores for admission.

5. NMAT by GMAC

NMIMS Management Aptitude Test (NMAT) is also one of the important MBA entrance exams. It has recently been acquired by GMAC and re-branded as NMAT by GMAC.

NMAT by GMAC has various candidate-friendly options. For instance, candidates can appear for the exam a total of three times and the best of three scores will be used for admission.

The NMAT by GMAC exam has three main sections:

- Language Skills
- Quantitative Skills
- Logical Reasoning

6. Management Aptitude Test (MAT)

MAT is also one of the most popular MBA entrance exams. More than 600 institutes accept MAT exam scores for admission to management programmes. Conducted by the All India Management Association (AIMA), MAT is held four times a year – February, May, September and December. The exam is held in both online (computer-based) and offline (written) mode. Held for 150 minutes, MAT question paper has 200 questions. The aspirant is tested on the following five areas:

- Indian and Global Environment
- Language Comprehension
- Data Analysis and Sufficiency
- Mathematical Skills
- Intelligence and Critical Reasoning

7. ATMA

ATMA is also a national-level management entrance test. It is conducted in online as well as offline mode and held four times a year-February, May, July and August. ATMA scores are used for admission in by several management programmes in over 600 MBA institutes. Held for three hours, ATMA question paper consists of the following sections:

- Analytical Reasoning Skills Part 1
- Analytical Reasoning Skills Part 2
- Quantitative Skills Part 1
- Quantitative Skills Part 2
- Verbal Skills Part 1
- Verbal Skills Part 2

8. IBSAT

ICFAI Business School Aptitude Test or IBSAT is an institute level entrance test. The exam is conducted by ICFAI Foundation for Higher Education. IBSAT exam scores are used for admission to MBA and Ph.D Programmes at nine ICFAI Business School (IBS) campuses

IBSAT exam is held over a period of 15 days wherein the candidate can book a slot as per convenience.

The computer-based test (CBT) assesses the applicant's ability in the following:

- Verbal Ability
- Reading Comprehension
- Quantitative Aptitude
- Data Adequacy and Data Interpretation

9. MAHA CET

Maharashtra Common Entrance Test is a state-level management entrance exam. The exam is conducted by the Directorate of Technical Education, Maharashtra, for admission to various management courses such as MMS, PGDBM and PGDM in various institutes in the state of Maharashtra.

MAH CET is generally held in the month of March. Candidates need to attempt 200 questions in 150 minutes. MAH-CET question paper has two sections:

Verbal Ability and Reading Comprehension

- Quantitative Aptitude
- Logical / Abstract Reasoning

10. IRMASAT

IRMASAT or IRMA Admission test is an institute-level entrance examination. It is conducted for admission to Post Graduate Diploma in Rural Management

(PRM) and Fellow Programme in Rural Management (FPRM) at IRMA exam is held in the month of January.

IRMA uses CAT/XAT scores for short-listing candidates in the first round. Shortlisted candidates are then called for IRMA written test or IRMASAT on the subject of "Issues of Social Concern". Candidates need to answer 40 questions in 80 minutes.

11. KITEE MBA

KITEE is also national-level computer-based test for multiple courses, one of them being MBA. The KITEE exam is conducted by Kalinga Institute of Industrial Technology in January every year. The exam scores are primarily used for admission for two programmes:

a) MBA at KITEE
b) MBA (Rural Management)

Candidates need to answer 150 questions in 150 minutes. There are four sections in KIITEE MBA:

12. OJEE MBA

Odisha Joint Entrance Exam or OJEE is a state-level MBA entrance test conducted by the Government of Orisha. The test scores are used for admission to various MBA courses in Odisha. The exam is conducted in the month of April-May. OJEE is a written test where candidates need to attempt 120 questions in 120 minutes. OJEE MBA has five sections to be attempted in two hours:

- Verbal reasoning
- Analytical reasoning
- General Knowledge
- Comprehension
- Computer and Business fundamentals

13. KMAT

Karnataka Management Aptitude Test or KMAT is also a state-level entrance examination for admission to post-graduate level programmes offered by MBA colleges and B-Schools in the state of Karnataka. KMAT exam is held thrice in the months of May, July and September. KMAT registration schedule is announced in April.

Conducted by Karnataka Private Post Graduate Colleges Association (KPPGCA), KMAT scores are used for admission by more than 169 colleges across the state.

Candidates need to attempt 120 questions in 120 minutes. KMAT consists of the following sections:

- Language Comprehension
- Mathematical Skills
- Basic Aptitude

14. APICET

Andhra Pradesh - Integrated Common Entrance Test orAPICET is a state-level MBA entrance examination conducted for admission to various B-Schools and MBA colleges in the state of Andhra Pradesh. APICET is generally held in the month of May. In 2019, the exam will be conducted by Sri Venkateshwara University, Tirupati, on behalf of Andhra Pradesh State Council of Higher Education (APSCHE).

15. TSICET

Telangana State Integrated Common Entrance Test or TSICET is a state-level written MBA entrance test. TSICET was held for the first time in May 2015. The test scores are used for admission to various MBA courses in the state of Telangana.

TSICET question paper has three sections:

- Analytical Ability
- Mathematical Ability
- Communication Ability

16. TANCET

Tamil Nadu Common Entrance Test or TANCET is a state-level written entrance examination conducted for admission to MBA courses in the state of Tamil Nadu. TANCET is conducted by Anna University, Chennai, on behalf of the Government of Tamil Nadu.

TANCET exam is held in May, is for two hours (100 questions) and tests the candidate's ability in:

- Analysis of Business Situations
- Reading Comprehension
- Quantitative Ability
- Data Sufficiency
- English Usage

17. TISSNET

Tata Institute of Social Sciences National Entrance Test or TISSNET is an institute-level exam conducted by Tata Institute of Social Sciences for all Masters programmes offered in IMHST, Chennai, MHAT, Calicut and G-SET, Ranchi. A computer-based exam, TISSNET is held for 100 minutes (1 hour and 40 minutes).

9

Pedagogical Change

Pedagogy refers more broadly to the theory and practice of education and how this influences the growth of learners. Pedagogy is the study of how knowledge and skills are exchange in an educational context and it considers the interactions that take place during learning. Pedagogies very greatly, as they reflect the different social, political, culture context from which they emerge. Conventional pedagogies view the teachers as knowledge holders and student as the recipient of knowledge.

The pedagogy adopted by teachers shape their actions, judgments and other teaching strategies by taking into consideration theories of learning, understandings of students and their needs, and the backgrounds and interests of individual students.

Management education as an academic discipline, has drawn from various other subjects such as economics, psychology, sociology, and history to develop its theoretical frameworks. The multi-disciplinary approach adopted mainly focused on managerial aspects of the business such as organisational behaviour, management decision-making, management communications, leaderships, etc. initially management curriculum covered besides general management theory and models, specialised main functional areas, such as marketing, finance and human resource management. Now the management education covers more functional areas like international business, operations, agri-business, supply chain management retail system and decision analysis, etc. in order to deliver specialised skills in management dimensions, the model envisaged aimed at maintaining a correct balance between theory and practical needs of business and also attaining the standards of academic rigor in theory and research.

In India, for management education, the IIMs became brand and bench mark for other management institutes in almost all aspects. They mostly followed IIM pedagogy in terms of course content, curriculum, quality, faculty, infrastructure, placements and institute – industry interface.

Management education, in-spite of its rapid development and popularity is now in a state of crisis (Shetty, NS).

Indian management education has been broadly following the American system American B-Schools have focus on US business environment. They evolved the management framework and pedagogy embedded in structural and functional arrangement of their system.

"While adopting US model no serious attempts have been made by Indian B-Schools to produce grounded and contextualised research and pedagogy to suit Indian business environment. This is evident in the almost uniformity of the curricular across management schools in India. In USA, the course structure and focus differ among B-Schools reflecting their distinct identities but not in India.

The Indian management education has not drawn on the business tradition and exiting business practices.

Working Group

The working Group on Management Education of National Knowledge Commission (2006-07) observed: 'The materials used for teaching are also not of relevance to the student background or living experiences in India. The focus on campus interviews, careers and jobs further detracts students from gaining a disciplinary understanding of the specialisations and society in which they have to innovate and be influential leaders'.

As pointed out by Kamal Choudhary "Management Education in India, along with other higher education has built an edifice of learning but has deprived it of its foundations—foundations rooted in the social, economic, political and cultural life of people (Quoted in Philips and Narayan, 1989).

Contemporary Relevance

The contemporary relevance of what is taught and the methodology used is critical issue to be looked into in management education. The business scenario is changing rapidly all over the world. The business models, organisational structure, business strategies required and decision-making process adopted in the past became outdated and irrelevant. It is essential that the curriculum is constantly adapted to cope up with the changes in the business world and meet the aspirations of the industry. With the IT revolution and globalisation, the business world also became more technology based and competitive. This would require different focus of business organisation and management system. With this ever changing business scenario, the corporation organisations have to come up with imaginative products and services, new business models and innovative ways of meeting market needs and people's expectations. The management education has to be, therefore, dynamic driven by changes in the business world, globalisation, technological revolution and pressing economic and social imperatives. If the management education has to become relevant, it has to adjust to the prevailing dynamics of the business world. It should be flexible to incorporate changing business models and knowledge. The fundamental transformation of Indian management education is, therefore, both necessary and inevitable in the present dynamics of the Indian business world.

Though there is no general consensus on what should be the ideal management education model, there is an on-going debate on what it should contain and what disciplines should be taught. Management education is evolved as distinctly different from other disciplines. It has to be practically relevant to business world. Since it is multi-dimensional, the management education has to be a multi-disciplinary course. In fact, the management itself as a discipline has; originally, evolved as outcome of various disciplines such as economics, psychology, sociology, anthropology, statistics, computer science, history and industrial engineering. Knowledge of these disciplines is essential for business management. Even in the functional areas of management such as marketing, finance and human resource management, inter-disciplinary offerings become essential ingredients.

The management education pedagogy should give insights into the entire spectrum of business management of today and future in the Indian context. Unfortunately, most of the B-Schools continue to teach the same thing, as they used to do earlier though the business world is undergoing fundamental mange. The academic curriculum needs to be upgraded keeping in mind the changing business scenario and needs of the corporate world. The curriculum should be dynamic and progressive.

10
Employability

The All Indian Council for Technical Education (AICTE), the apex government body providing accreditation to MBA and Post Graduate Diploma in Business (PGDM) programmes across India, has pegged the number of business schools offering MBA in India at 3644. Additionally, there are 308 institutions offering PGDM programmes in India.

As India's economy started to boom, many entrepreneurs established their own B-Schools anticipating a surge in demand for professionally trained management graduates. According to AICTE, a whopping 927 B-Schools were established in the country between 2007 and 2012.

But, over the last few years, many B-Schools, especially the mid and bottom-tier ones, have been shutting shop. According to a report published in the *Times of India*, 147 B-Schools and MBA programmes offered by engineering institutions across the country closed down in the 2013-14 academic year.

The economic slowdown that India has been experiencing is one reason for many of these B-Schools closing their gates permanently. Many found it unfeasible to continue operations in the face of dying demand. Others, without proper facilities, solid faculty, and outdated curricula, have also been rendered unviable.

Added to that is a growing realisation among recruiters of the mediocre quality of education imparted at some of these B-Schools.

Instead of grabbing the lowest hanging fruit, recruiters are now concentrating on hiring management professionals exclusively from top-rung B-Schools even if they cost more, leaving the mid and the bottom-tier ones struggling to fill up seats.

Failing Employability

One of the impacts of the falling demand for MBA programmes at mid and bottom-tier B-Schools is the lowering employability of students graduating from these courses. As these schools began to experience a fall in demand for seats, they slackened their admission criteria resulting in virtually any graduate getting into these institutions. This resulted in an overall fall in the standards of MBA graduates leading to their low employability.

In a hard hitting report published in the Economic Times, it was revealed that a mere 10 per cent of B-School graduates are actually employable. According to the report, India produces about three lakh management graduates annually, but hardly 35,000 of them are employable.

Quoting the 2012 National Employability Report, Aspiring Minds, a talent assessment company, released a press brief highlighting the dismally low employability of India MBA graduates. According to the press release, the employability of MBA graduates from the class of 2011 was below 10 per cent for functional roles in the field of HR, marketing, and finance.

When it came to specialised roles like business consulting and analyst functions, which require exceptional English and cognitive skills, the employability of B-School graduates was even lower at 2.5 per cent and 7.9 per cent respectively.

The employability for customer service roles, in which the behavior and personality of graduates have a key role to play, hovered around 16 per cent. Employability in the area of operations was a little more than 15 per cent, while the same for the BPO/ITES sector was around 33 per cent.

Reasons for Low Employability

According to an Associated Chambers of Commerce and Industry of India (ASSOCHAM) paper on "B-Schools and Engineering Colleges shut down- Big Business Struggles," B-Schools barring the IIMs are fast losing their shine for corporate India Inc. The paper reveals that since 2009, campus recruitments at B-Schools have gone down by 40 per cent.

Some key reasons for this low employability of B-School graduates in the recent years include excess supply, lack of basic skills, lesser work experience of candidates, inexperienced faculty, and lack of practical and problem solving skills of graduates.

- *Excess Supply*: According to the ASSOCHAM paper "B-Schools and Engineering Colleges shut down- Big Business Struggles," MBA seats in India grew almost four-fold from 95,000 in 2006-07 to 3, 60,000 in 2011-12, resulting in a five-year CAGR of 30 per cent. While MBAs are graduating in lakhs every year, the annual requirement for managerial candidates in the Indian market is between 35,000 and 40,000. The MBA capacity in the country was built based on the projection of a 9 to 10 per cent economic growth rate. But with the economic growth slowing down over the past few years, job opportunities for MBAs have not grown in the same proportion leading to a supply that is much in excess of demand. J. Philip, the former director of IIM-Bengaluru and current director of the Xavier Institute of Management and Entrepreneurship, Bengaluru, was quoted as saying in an Economic Times article that India is the only country that could supply managers to European countries, most of which are facing a crunch.

- *Poor quality*: In a bid to increase the quantity of business schools in the country, the government and AICTE have been guilty of compromising on quality. According to Parag Kelkar, Director of Singhad Institute of Business Administration and Computer Application, Pune, institutes have been given approval without examining or inspecting documents, infrastructure, faculty, and other basic requirements. Four Market research firm Crisil published a report in 2014 estimating that tier-3 and tier-4 B-Schools together account for about 85 per cent of intake capacity of B-Schools in India. But these schools are riddled with massive problems in terms of infrastructure, qualified faculty members, and industry tie-ups.
- *Lack of basic skills*: T N Swaminathan, Director, branding and alumni relations, Great Lakes Institute of Management, in an interview with English news daily Times of India, said that many B-Schools are following university curriculum that is outdated. The same article quoted educational consultant Moorthy Selvakumaran as saying that many of the management courses run by engineering institutions do not focus on improving the skills of the candidates and making them employable.6 MBA graduates from many institutions lack even the most basic skills such as conversation, interviewing, CV writing, and proper dress sense. Many of them also lack the interpersonal and soft skills that are required to manage diverse teams working in different geographical locations, as is the case with organisations these days. At a time when B-Schools should be focusing on providing their students global skills and preparing them for employment in a global market, the lack of even these basic skills brings down their employability drastically.
- *Under-qualified faculty*: The impact of a highly qualified and well-connected faculty on MBA students cannot be emphasised enough. Unfortunately, many B-Schools in India have failed to attract good quality teaching staff into their folds. Many of these faculty members join a management institution immediately after completing their post-graduation and lack the industry experience and exposure that would go miles in helping their students. Most of these faculty members are also not permanent staff, but form part of the visiting faculty at many B-Schools. While B-Schools are guilty of ignoring the need to re-train their faculty, most of the teachers themselves don't make the effort of keeping themselves updated and work towards forming a network of industry linkages that might benefit their students.
- *Lesser work experience*: Another problem that is typical to Indian MBA graduates and Indian B-Schools, especially the ones that have relaxed admission criteria, is candidates' lack of experience. While in the U.S. and

Europe, it's almost impossible to get into a good B-School without some work experience, many students in India apply for admission to an MBA programme straight after graduation. This puts them at a disadvantage as they lack the industry exposure needed to draw maximum benefit out of their course. Their lack of experience and relatively young age when they graduate out of B-School lowers their employability even further.

Improving Employability

In its paper, ASSOCHAM has advised B-Schools to improve their infrastructure, train their faculty, pay well in order to attract good teachers, work on forming industry linkages, and spend money on research and knowledge creation to improve the employability of their graduates and hence draw more students into their fold.

Here are some measures that can be taken by B-Schools to improve the employability of their MBA students:

- Focus on skill building: B-Schools are advised not to underplay the significance of soft skills in improving the employability of their students. From encouraging creative thinking in their students to helping them build interpersonal and leadership skills to providing them with a global perspective of managing business – B-Schools need to do all this and more to improve the employability of their graduates. In fact, core "employability skills" should be integrated into the framework of their programme with enough time and platforms provided to the students to practice them.
- Update curriculum: B-Schools need to reinvent their core syllabus to stay relevant to the current times. Even if they have to follow a university dictated broad curriculum, they should be open to tweaking it or adding courses in order to add value for both students and employers.
- Explore MBA internship: Kul Bhushan Saxena, Professor Emeritus at Fortune Institute of International Business, floats the idea of enhancing the employability of fresh MBA graduates, who have no prior work experience through internships. According to him, internships offer an excellent way of connecting theory to real life and provide a real opportunity for experiential learning. As student-interns encounter the real complexities involved in running a business, they develop both skills and attitude key to their success in the corporate world.
- Re-train faculty: As advised by ASSOCHAM in its paper, B-Schools need to have a budget for updating and re-training their faculty in emerging global business perspectives. They should also encourage their faculty members to take refresher courses, study breaks, and participate in industry events to keep abreast of the latest trends in the world of business.

- Equal focus on practical knowledge: While it's important to impart theoretical knowledge to MBA students, it should not be done at the cost of practical problem solving skills. An employer is unlikely to miss the lack of practical experience in trouble-shooting real world business problems in a candidate. Therefore, it's not just imperative to impart practical knowledge to students, but also give them enough opportunities to test their problem solving skills.
- Open more specialisation streams: Most MBA programmes offer specialisation in conventional streams like HR, marketing, finance, operations, IT, etc. With a growing need for management professionals in almost every kind of business, B-Schools should consider opening up more specialisation streams like healthcare, education, analytics, etc. This will improve the employability of their graduates in their chosen field by several notches.
- Make entrepreneurs, not employees: T N Swaminathan, in his interview to Times of India, said that business schools should focus on making entrepreneurs. Their emphasis should be on creating job providers, not seekers. It's also a well-known fact that many employers look for an entrepreneurial attitude in their employees, so a focus on this aspect will automatically improve the candidate's brand value.

Campus placement plays a vital role in deciding the prominence of the university. What kind of companies come for placements and how employable or industry ready the fresh graduates adds to the credibility of an educational institute.

Global University Employability Ranking, 2018, published by Times Higher Education (THE) offered the latest rankings of top lists the top 150 institutions for employability based on a survey of 7,000 major employers around the world.

India's Best

The list includes three Indian institutes — the Indian Institute of Science (IISç), Bengaluru at 28th position globally while the Indian Institute of Technology(IIT), Delhi jumped 92 ranks higher from last year and made it to 53rd most employable institute in the world. Indian Institute of Management (IIM), Ahmedabad, made a debut in the list making a market, 144th position.

Rise of the Dragon

Despite the presence of three institutes from India and a climb of almost 100 points, India sun lags behind China. The Land of *Dragons* has seven universities in the list, including *Peking* University at the 19th spot.

The year was great for Asia as closer to home destinations -Japan and Singapore made it to top 10 institutes. The University of Tokyo, Japan secured 9th and National University of Singapore seemed 10th spot.

Fall of the Brit

The western education institutes continue to find place in the top 10 list with United States of America(USA) leading with top three most employable institutes Harvard University, California Institute of Technology, MIT, respectively.

British universities struggle to make it in the top list, thanks to Brexit, even as Cambridge University was ranked at 4th spot. Singapore and Japan made a mark in the top 10, while the UK had five universities listed in top 50.Germany, on the other hand has almost doubled the number.

Rank 2018	*Institution*	*Country*
1	Harvard University	United States
2	California Institute of Technology	United States
3	Massachusetts Institute of Technology	United States
4	University of Cambridge	United Kingdom
5	Stanford University	United States
6	Technical University of Munich	Germany
7	Princeton University	United States
8	Yale University	United States
9	The University of Tokyo	Japan
10	National University of Singapore	Singapore

Suggestions for Improving the Employability Quotient

The following are the suggestions which the management education institutions need to focus on:

- Industry- Institute collaboration in the areas of curriculum, teaching, research and training.
- Industry relevant courses need to design, to improve the students' basic skills by educating them using the right methodology.
- To build a proper system to check their basic level of knowledge and train them accordingly.
- Proper selection procedure to recruit quality faculty
- Formation of global networks of innovation for research and scholarship

- Leaders/ Heads of the institution need to be oriented for creating a learning environment and proper work culture.
- Students need to be given proper goal setting orientation at the beginning of the course.
- Faculty to assist the students in the right direction after they are clear about their goals. Faculty development programmes need to be taken seriously and implemented.
- Faculty to be encouraged to take up consultancy works with industry
- Proper evaluation methods to evaluate the skills of the students need to be taken up.
- Students need to encourage to participate in the extra-curricular activities line online activities, events, paper presentations, workshops etc.
- Students need to have strong career path in their mind, be clear about what they want to do and to focus on one job at a time. Hence, career development programmes need to be taken up by the institutes
- Students need to be counselled by Professors, seniors, placement officers on regular basis.
- Innovation labs need to be established to create working space where industry, academics, and students can develop, test their new ideas and get trained in creative skills and finally link with start-ups.
- Social responsibility activities need to be focused to inculcate values.

11

Aptitudes and Skills

Today, management education should aim at developing a holistic personality capable of maintaining a balance among contradictory demands, taking charge of functional responsibilities, being accountable for one's action, and contributing to create a desirable future for businesses in particular and the economy as a whole. The ultimate goal of management education is to prepare students to achieve professional success in business management. Keeping in view this larger purpose of management education, business schools should thus focus on developing a number of aptitudes and skills, as given by Natashaa Kaul:

1. Management Schools should provide an education that combines both generalist and specialist components.
2. Management Education should be much more holistic in character. It needs to be more integrated — incorporating a number of functional, quantitative, non-quantitative and analytical fields including the humanities and sciences — to educate the "whole" manager to meet the responsibilities and challenges of the future.
3. Management Schools, thus, should aim to develop future managers with a "portfolio of capabilities" quantitative, computer and other analytical skills, functional knowledge and communications, interpersonal, bargaining, negotiation, entrepreneurship, administration and other non-cognitive skills.
4. Management Education involves a lifetime process — a "continuum of learning" — with self-teaching and initiative beyond the business school, work experience, on-the-job training, and management at the corporate level and possibly refurbishment of management knowledge at business schools at least once during a career.
5. Management Schools should teach more effective environmental scanning and analysis which is particularly important for domestic and international business.
6. A closer partnership should be developed between educators and managers in future.
7. Management Schools should strive to develop experiential courses in creativity and managerial innovation.

8. Develop state-of-the-art domain knowledge, skills and competencies.
9. Impart generic skills transferable across domains and situations — creativity, innovation, problem-solving, strategic thinking and communication.
10. Build thinking-ability skills and emphasise cognitive development (conceptualisation, analysis, synthesis) dealing with abstraction.
11. Foster a spirit of inquiry and critical evaluation of and experimentation with new ideas, information, approaches, assumptions and frames of reference.
12. Inculcate research ability, research value, and methodological rigor.
13. Cultivate one's ability to learn on one's own and instigate learning how to learn, autonomous learning, life-long learning and one's ability to reflect one's own learning process.
14. Promote original thinking and the critical examination of prevailing concepts as opposed to merely conforming to existing notions and approaches.
15. Generate cross-functional perspectives and mind sets, systemic orientation, and system thinking.
16. Build one's ability to convert ideas into practice – delineating, planning, implementing and evaluating ideas and concepts.
17. Instill professional and human values.
18. Further the right and relevant attitude to grow and learn and an openness to change.
19. Teach behavioral skills like cooperation, collaboration, team work and inter-personal competence.
20. Breed entrepreneurial leadership-like initiatives, risk taking, mobilising support and resources, and self-discipline.
21. Instill a transcendental ability such as vision, aspiration, transformation, or inspiration.
22. Develop self-efficacy, positive self-regard, self-directing and self-regulating capabilities, positive outcome judgment.
23. Focalise on integrated personality development, congruency among values, attitudes, thoughts, feeling and actions, and integrity.
24. Create an understanding of the societal context and sensitivity to social developmental issues.
25. Imbue the holistic perspective by way of a balanced emphasis on often conflicting constituents of the system within the framework of the larger purpose of life and society.

Viswanathan Bharatan and Mangalaguri Deshmuk listed the following skills required for Management Students:

1. *Technical skills required*
    - Technology Trends
    - Application – Domains
    - Engineering Concepts
    - Standards
    - Tools and Technique
    - Operating Machinery
    - Equipment
    - Computer Literacy
    - Web Literacy
2. *Business skills required*
    - Entrepreneurship
    - Profit and Loss
    - Budgeting and Costing
    - Business plans
    - Financial Accounting
3. *Industry awareness skills required*
    - Industry types
    - Industry Dynamics
    - Services
    - Products
    - Vision, Mission, Strategy, Goals
    - Culture
    - Balance Sheets/ P and L
4. *Soft Skills Required*
    - Attitudes
    - Enthusiasm
    - Ethics and Value System
    - Inter Personal Relationships
    - Team Work
    - Leadership
5. *Process Skills Required*
    - Project Life Cycle
    - Product and Services
    - Project Management
    - Quality Assurance
    - Customer Satisfaction
    - Productivity
    - Standards and Metrics

- Procedures and Guidelines Problem Solving Skills Required
- Problem Definition
- Thinking Skills
- Comprehension
- Analytical Skills
- Logical Skills
- Simulation and Modeling
- Planning
- Designing

6. *Creative Skills Required*
   - Innovation
   - Lateral Thinking
   - Creativity
   - Visualisation
   - Aesthetics
7. *Communication Skills Required*
   - Active Listening
   - Verbal
   - Speed Reading
   - Use of Body Language
   - Presentation
   - Communication Styles
   - Coaching, Mentoring
   - Quick Typing
8. *Organising Skills Required*
   - Manage Time, Energy, Resources and Risk
   - Prioritise Work
   - Sort Data/ Object
   - Identify and analyse alternatives and take Decisions
   - Predict, Monitor and Control Outcomes
9. *Thinking Skills Required*
   - Systems Thinking
   - Lateral thinking
   - Creative thinking
10. *Presentation Skills Required*
    - Language
    - Logical Flow
    - Poise/ Body Language
    - Clarity

- Tone and Volume
- Use of Visuals
- Tools and Demonstrations

11. *Interpersonal Skills Required*
    - Personal Styles/ Profiles
    - Leadership/ Follower-ship
    - Trust and Faith
    - Giving and Taking Feedback
    - Other person's Views
    - Self-knowledge
12. *Team work Skills Required*
    - Importance of Teams
    - Purpose
    - Place
    - Power
    - Plan
    - People
    - Process
    - Performance
13. *Personal Productivity Skills Required*
    - Personal Mastery
    - Soft Skills
    - Time Management
    - Prioritise
    - Organise
    - Attention to Details
14. *Life-long Learning Skills Required*
    - Need for lifelong learning
    - Learning styles
    - Learning techniques
    - Tools
15. *Attitudes Required*
    - Enthusiasm
    - Ethics and Integrity
    - Professionalism
    - Friendly and Collaborative
    - Commitment
    - Responsive
    - Proactive

The primary need of business school is to prepare student to become leaders and managers, and hence design courses in a way that students acquire the essential managerial skills.

To handle complex managerial assignments students should also become competent in the applying these skills. This is really necessary because the growth and successes of an organisation may get affected because of a dearth of managers with the necessary skills. A recent study based on a survey of senior managers, conformed that successful or unsuccessful managerial performance is related to either the presence or absence of these three skills among the managers.

Various students and their reviews have confirmed that intrinsic motivation, interest, engagement in learning, and perceived competence among college students can be promoted through autonomy, conversely when students perceive that they are being controlled. They may perform poorly or experience reduced intrinsic motivation. *Autonomy-enhancing behaviour* as opposed to *autonomy-suppressing behaviour* must be incorporated in the classroom design.

The classroom focus needs to move from *teaching* to *learning*. Teaching is controlled and driven by the instructor, whereas learning is student centered, which requires it to be responsive and customised.

We all operate and learn in *permanent white water* (PWW) conditions-environments characterised by novel, messy, costly, surprising and unpreventable events. The two most important elements necessary for successful managerial leadership learning in PWW are (a) *self-directed learning,* where the learner has substantial control over the purpose, the form, the content, and the pace of learning, and (b) *expressive learning* (learning through the process of expression).

Developing Management Skills Learning Model
(Whetton and Cameron)

Skill assessment:	Diagnostic survey and experience logs (What do I need to Improve?)
Skill learning:	Subject matter: Translation of research into behavioural guidelines (What are the best bets for handling difficulty management responsibility?)
Skill analysing:	Cases (According to the behavioral guidelines, what happened and why?)
Skill practice:	Role-plays and exercise (How am I doing in my efforts to improve?)
Skill application:	Transfer of learning into everyday practice (How am I going to apply what I've learned?)

The paradigm shift from a teacher centric process to student learning focus involves asking questions like what the student needs to learn is it sync with what the industry demands. Eliciting student discovery and construction of knowledge is the responsibility of the faculty and it creates pressure on the faculty to produce learning. One important shift in the learning focus is the realisation that teaching is complex and hence requires effort on the part of the faculty to learn the art and the institution need to invest time and resource to develop the faculty resources capable of delivering value. Learning is a natural process of growth. The direction in which the growth takes place is determined chiefly by the interests, curiosities, and needs felt by the individual. Team teaching is considered to be more efficacious than individual teaching. Few important points to be kept in mind for team teaching are listed below by Young and Kram;

Faculty-Team Learning

- Acknowledge the learning curve
- Relinquish the role of expert
- Support individual learning
- Take time to discuss group process before, during, and after the team teaching experience

Staffing

- Create mix team of veterans and new-comers
- Seek volunteers
- Modify workload accounting
- Use part-time faculty
- Create incentives for continued team teaching

Systemic Support

- Modify performance appraisal and reward systems
- Create structured opportunities for learning from experience
- Document and discuss best practice
- Adapt administrative structures to support team teaching

12

Concerns

The Government of India has appointed various committees time to time to take a critical review of management education in India. The National Knowledge Commission (NKC) was established by the Prime Minister of India in 2005. The commission had appointed a working group on management education under the chairmanship of Prof. S. L. Rao.

This working group had referred various reports on management education since 1991 and along with the existing state of business education in India like

1. Kurian Committee Report - 1991.
2. Ishwar Dayal Committee Report - 2001.
3. The Management Education Review Committee Report - 2003.
4. U.R.Rao Report on Faculty Development Programme - 2004,
5. All India Management Association (AIMA) Document prepared in 2005

After going through the various reports and existing state of business education in India, the committee has observed that the Indian management education is still facing a number of challenges e.g.

1. Though, India produces a large number of graduates perhaps next to US, but still a scholarly debate on curriculum pedagogy and innovation is negligible.
2. Most institutes depend on curricula and materials developed elsewhere and have not developed on intrinsic capacity to respond and evolve to changing needs of various sectors of industry.
3. Many institutions still are unable to fulfill the mandatory changes imposed on them, such as upgrading of the curriculum by the universities or the board of management studies.
4. Management institutions in India are today estimated to be graduating approximately one lac (+) students annually. However, what proportion of the total requirement will be for the increasing more expensive graduates in management and what proportion would be for the less expensive lower levels of managers is not yet clear. Again there is a need to raise the number from the current level of one lac (+) managers to about 3 lacs (+) managers a year over the next 10 -15 years.

5. With the opening up of trade and cross border movement of goods and services, the country needs a paradigm shift in management education and management training for working professionals.
6. Presently, management education is treated as sub-department of engineering by AICTE rather than recognising that management itself. The working group recommends a fully autonomous governing council for management education.

On the basis of the various reports and the present status of Management Education Goutam G. Saha of MGM's Institute of Management, Aurangabad identified certain major issues and concerns of Indian Management Education. Let us see some of these.

1) *Ensuring Quality Research:* In view of the establishment of a large number of institutes, qualified staff are not readily available. At present many faculty members are without Ph.D and research experience. In fact, UGC expects either Ph.D or Net/Set as an essential qualification for the positions of lecturers, but due to shortage of faculty at college/ university level, simple Master's Degree holders are becoming teachers of Management Education Institutes. Industry experience is also not insisted for selection of teachers. Moreover AICTE has no mechanism to provide training to the newly recruited staff for Management Education Institutions. Most of the newly recruited staff members adopt only lecture method in classrooms. New faculty members cannot take up research work and teaching materials development activities. Teaching is mostly on the traditional model.
2) *Promoting Research Culture:* Many management education institutes do not have research culture. Research is a critical and creative activity undertaken on systematic discipline based and dedicated to increasing knowledge. Research can contribute to knowledge through innovative idea and techniques, conceptual refinements or constructive critiques and syntheses. The tradition of research in Indian Management Education is not very strong and sound.
3) *Developing Staff:* To create good and competent teachers for B-Schools, the staff/faculty development programmes must be developed and implemented. Presently, the teachers try to grow without any rationality. Recently, AICTE informed the managements of Management Education Institutes to depute their faculty to attend Faculty Development Programmes available at select institutions. But no serious attention is given to this and AICTE is helpless in this.
4) *Developing Relevant Reading Material:* Many of the textbooks prescribed for Indian Management Education students are written by Management scholars and researches in America, Britain, Japan, Germany etc. They are

written in their national contexts and relevant to their industrial, business and government. There is a need to have books and study materials to our society and economic structure.

5) *Promoting Interaction with Industry:* Expecting a few top ranking B-Schools, Management Institutes have a very little interface with industries, businesses and public and private enterprises. The main strength of top class B-Schools like Kellog, Wharton, Sloan and Harvard is their strong and close relationship with industry through teaching, research, student placement, problem solving and case study preparation. Indian situation needs to change in the interaction with industry. Some of the Indian institutions like— ICFAI Hyderabad, MDI Gurugram, XLRI Jamshedpur and Wellingkar Mumbai—are ahead of other institutions in term of interaction with industry. There is an immediate need to change the situation of interface between education institutions and industries businesses in India.
6) *Evolving Proper Accreditation and Rating System*: The rapid expansion of Management Institutes needs a specialised agency to accredit them. AICTE is a big body with many responsibilities and is unable to satisfactorily carry out the function of accreditation of Management Institutes. The National Knowledge Commission (NKC) recommended rating as an additional measure to inform the students, the parents and the public of the quality of Management Education in view of mushrooming growth of business schools in India, many of which do not meet even the minimum requirements of the acceptable quality. Information on rating would be a great service to all stake-holders.
7) *Creating Independent Body:* Management education must be a concern of a body exclusively for Management Education. AICTE is unable to monitor the functioning of Management Institutes as it has several other functions. All India Management Association is of the opinion that there is a need for all India Council for Management Education, independent of AICTE.
8) *Promoting Corporate Governance:* Presently, many Business Schools lack corporate governance system. There is a need to have independent Directors to implement decisions of the Audit Committee. B-Schools should become process driven. Corporate governance should become a part of accreditation. Faculty development as well as involvement in the administration needs to be a part of corporate governance.
9) *Broadening Specialisations:* A variety of subjects are becoming popular in the society. These subjects need to be studied so that the management of these subject areas get systematic and scientific orientation. Agricultural Management, Hospital Management, Small Scale Industries management have become popular and are growing in terms of materials development, teaching capabilities, etc.

10) *Creating Global Mindset:* In the present day globalisation scenario, industry needs executives with multifaceted talent. How to inculcate global mindset in the executives is very important. Internationalisation of business makes it necessary to have different knowledge and skills.

11) *Developing Internationalisation*: As business is getting global day by day there is an increasing need for Management schools to produce global managers. Indian Management Education should be more global. Hence,

- The business schools must admit international students to the programme. The Indian management institutes are the only ones with no international participation.
- The B-Schools should induct a few international faculties and provide an opportunity to the students to listen about other country's business culture and systems.
- The B-Schools should provide an active programme of students and faculty exchange with advanced countries.
- To ensure that at least 25 per cent of the curriculum deals with international subjects like International Economics, International Marketing, International Financial Management or International Business Management etc.
- Indian B-Schools should collaborate with some well-known foreign B-Schools by which Indian students can do part of their education in those institutes.
- The B-Schools also collaborate with some foreign placement consultancies to make sure at least some students can obtain jobs abroad.

Multifold Agenda

Indian Management Education should have the following multifold agenda as suggested by R. Anita, well experienced teacher of Management.

- Contribute to National development
- Focus on entrepreneurial orientation to inculcate the entrepreneurial skills
- Foster Global competencies among future managers
- Inculcate values and sense of social responsibility
- Sharpen analytical and problem- solving capabilities
- Enrich students with emotional, spiritual and intellectual intelligence
- Build sustainable competitive edge through research by creating knowledge.
- Aligned to corporate requirements
- Ultimately, develop as centers of excellence

Why Prefer Management Education?

Over the globe organisations and individuals prefers Management education because

- Management education facilitates access to opportunity and wealth creation to an increasingly diverse population.
- Management education contributes directly to society by facilitating economic development and service.
- Management education provides a fertile environment for the development and incubation of new ideas.
- Management education leads to the creation of knowledge essential to the success of 21st century organisations.
- Management education produces cutting edge ideas and theories that help to advance organisational efficiency and effectiveness.
- Management education provides significant life-long economic benefit to graduates.
- Management education provides graduates with a portfolio of competencies that facilitates meaningful contributions to organisation engaged in a variety of enterprises and pursuits.
- Management education produces well-rounded graduates who can help to strengthen the connection between business and society.

Revitalisation Need

Management Education in India is facing multiple issues. However, proliferation of Management Schools, quality of education, faculty storage, poor regulatory mechanism and governance and accountabilities are major concerns.

Management Education in the country need to be revitalised in order to meet the expectations of all the key stakeholders such as students, faculty, society, industry, government and global community at large. Hence it is imperative that the ever growing crisis of relevance vis-à-vis Management Education is addressed collectively, enabling key stakeholders to contribute their mite in the process and system improvements. A broad based consultation with the stakeholders might help in developing a holistic framework for effective Management Education. It is time to collectively reflect and take stock so that we are ready for next wave in Management Education.

Why India Needs Management Skills?

- India and the Indians have undergone a paradigm shift. There have been fundamental and irreversible changes in the economy, government policies, outlook of business and industry, and in the mindset of the Indians in general.

- From a shortage economy of food and foreign exchange, India has now become a surplus one.
- From an agro-based economy, India has emerged as a service oriented one.
- From the low-growth of the past, the economy has become a high-growth one in the long-term.
- Having been an aid recipient, India is now joining the aid givers club.
- Although India was late and slow in modernisation of industry in general in the past, it is now a frontrunner in the emerging Knowledge based New Economy.
- The Government is continuing its reform and liberalisation not out of compulsion but out of conviction.
- Indian companies are no longer afraid of Multinational Companies. They have become globally competitive and many of them have become MNCs themselves.
- Fatalism and contentment of the Indian mindset have given way to optimism and ambition.
- Introvert and defensive approach have been replaced by outward-looking and, confident attitude.
- In place of denial and sacrifice, the Indian value system has started recognising seeking of satisfaction and happiness.
- The Indian culture, which looked down upon wealth as a sin and believed in simple living and high thinking, has started recognising prosperity and success as acceptable and necessary goals.
- Indian management graduates no longer queue up for safe government jobs. They prefer and enjoy the challenges and risks of becoming entrepreneurs and global players in the emerging private sectors.

To Innovate Change

The quality of management education very much depends upon the combined efforts of the educational system as a whole, the educational institutions and the teaching faculty. Quality can be upgraded only when these pillars are equally efficient and collaborative Management.

Education Institutions are already experimenting with different approaches to address some, if not all, of these challenges. But further strategies are needed by the institutions. Proper leadership in the Institutions, inspiring faculty, students having learning aptitude will make a difference in the student exit quality. Innovation is critical to growth of the country by finding solutions to key global challenges. Hence it is the responsibility of the business schools to innovate and change accordingly to produce ethical, creative, talented and independent thinking leaders.

Quality

The following are some of the suggestions for the development of quality of Management education made in the *International Journal of Research in Economics and Social Science*, May 2016

- Industry-Institute collaboration inthe areas of curriculum, teaching, research and training.
- Industry relevant courses need to design.
- To improve the students basic skills by educating them using the right methodology.
- To build a proper system to check their basic level of knowledge and train them accordingly.
- Proper selection procedure to recruit quality faculty.
- Formation of global networks of innovation for research and scholarship.
- Leaders/ Heads of the institution need to be oriented for creating a learning environment and proper work culture.
- Students need to be given proper goal setting orientation at the beginning of the course.
- Faculty to assist the students in the right direction after they are clear about their goals.
- Faculty development programmes need to take seriously and implemented.
- Faculty to be encouraged to take up consultancy works with industry.
- Proper evaluation methods to evaluate the skills of the students need to be taken up.
- Students need to encouraged to participate in the extra-curricular activities like online activities, events, paper presentations, workshops etc.
- Students need to have strong career path in their mind, be clear about what they want to do and to focus on one job at a time. Hence, career development programmes need to be taken up by the institutes.
- Students need to be counseled by Professors, seniors, placement officers on regular basis.
- Innovation labs need to be established to create working space where industry, academics and students can develop, test their new ideas and get trained in creative skills and finally link with start-ups.
- Social responsibility activities need to be focused to inculcate values.

Emerging Concerns

Indian B-Schools are not untouched by the contractual compulsions of management education in the international arena. Indeed B-Schools in India are facing multiple issues such as proliferation of B-Schools, quality of education, faculty shortage, poor regulatory mechanism and governance and accountability. Shweta and Manoj Kumar in their article in the *Journal of Management and Public Policy* (December 2011) analyse the issues and challenges of management education in the emerging scenario and remarkable insights into revitalising B-Schools.

Proliferation of B-Schools: Management education in India started in early 1950 with a noble purpose of creating a professional cadre of managers to run the businesses and become entrepreneurs. Initially the growth of B-Schools was very slow. According to National Knowledge Commission, the growth rate of B-Schools rose to alarming level Promoters of B-Schools cared little about infrastructure and intellectual capital while indulging in unmindful expansion. Indeed, proliferation of B-Schools has defeated the noble purpose of Management education in India. A large number of B-Schools are run as teaching shops without good quality faculty and adequate infrastructure conducive for learning.

Quality of Education: An important function of Business schools is to develop relevant knowledge serve as a source of critical thought and inquiry unfortunately, most of the B-Schools have thrived on marketing gimmicks and advertising budget rather than intellectual endeavours. The Government of India (GOI) formed the All India Council of Technical Education (AICTE), a statutory body under the Ministry of Human Resources to regulate the functioning of technical institutes in India. AICTE has given full autonomy to the B-Schools vis-a-vis curriculum development, assessment of students, conduct of examination, recruitment of faculty, tuition fee etc. However, there are no checks and balances on these matters.

Working Group on Management Education of National Knowledge Commission (2006-07) rightly observes: The materials used for teaching are also not of relevance to the student background or living experiences in India. The focus on campus interviews, careers and jobs further detracts students from gaining a disciplinary understanding of the specialisation and society in which they have to innovate and be influential leaders. Report of the working Group also draws attention towards negligible debate on curriculum, pedagogy and innovation in Management education as well as lack of inherent capabilities of the institutions to address the evolving needs of various stakeholders by upgrading and refining their courses. The scenario has spiraling impact which is reflected in the low employability of Management graduates. Indian B-Schools are not exhibiting any significant initiative to improve the quality of education. There has hardly been any conference on quality of Management education in last several years.

Faculty Shortage: Storage of qualified faculty in Indian B-Schools is major concern. Currently the institutions are facing 30 per cent shortage of faculty and it might rise up to 50 per cent by 2020 if the scenario does not improve.

There are good number of doctoral research programmes in Management except the Fellow Programme in Management of IIMS and Ph.Ds programmes of IITs.

National Knowledge Commission's Working Group on Management Education advocates a greater role of industry in promoting research programmes in B-Schools as they are the major beneficiaries in terms of steady supply of efficient manpower. Indeed, the industry can sponsor research programmes set up dedicated research chair professorships in specific domains, grant fellowships to doctoral candidates and open their gates for collaborative research projects. Besides, the corporate houses may also encourage some of their senior professionals to participate in research programmes and pursue higher education. B-Schools are unlikely to handle the shortage of faculty without active support from industry.

Poor Regulatory Mechanism: All India Council for Technical Education (AICTE) regulates Management education in India. National Knowledge Commission has truthfully observed: ...there are several instances where an engineering college or a Business school is approved, promptly, in a small house of a metropolitan suburb without the requisite teachers, infrastructure or facilities, but established universities experience difficulties in obtaining similar approvals.

Of late, the AICTE has started cleansing its regulatory mechanism by using a transparent online disclosure system. However, the regulatory mechanism remains inadequate due to misplaced focus on infrastructure and faculty-student ratio. Besides, AICTE does not have resources to check the accuracy of the mandatory disclosures although its team visits institutions in different regions randomly.

Governance and Accountability: Most of the private B-Schools in India offering Post Graduate Diploma in Management are managed by charitable trusts registered under Indian Trust Act 1908 or educational societies registered under Societies Registration Act 1860. In case of charitable trusts, the trustees are generally from the same family having absolute powers to manage the affairs of the institutions. The trustees hold the office for the whole life and hence cannot be removed for their indulgences or mis-governance or incompetence. So is the case of educational societies where majority of founding members belong to the same family. Thus the governing bodies of B-Schools have unlimited power and authority without concomitant responsibility. AICTE concerned about compliance of the regulatory norms and hence governance and accountability do not feature in its relations with the B-Schools.

B-Schools in India need to revitalise Management education in the country in order to meet the expectations of all the key stakeholders such as students, faculty, society, industry, government and global community at large. Hence it is imperative that the ever-growing crisis of relevance vis-a-vis Management education is addressed collectively, enabling key-stakeholders to contribute their mite in the process and system improvements. A broad-based consultation with the stakeholders might help in developing a holistic framework for effective Management education of governance and accountability.

Challenges

- Though, India produces a large number of graduates perhaps next to U.S. but still a scholarly debate on curriculum pedagogy and innovation is negligible.
- Most institutes depend on curricula and materials developed elsewhere and have not developed on intrinsic capacity to respond and evolve to changing needs of various sectors of industry.
- Many institutions still are unable to fulfill the mandatory changes imposed on them, such as upgrading of the curriculum by the universities or the board of management studies.
- With the opening up of trade and cross border movement of goods and services, the country needs a paradigm shift in management education and management training for working professionals.
- Presently, management education is treated as sub department of engineering by AICTE rather than recognising that management itself. The working group recommends a fully autonomous governing council for management education.
- The current curriculum in management education does not teach students in facing the challenges in business environment.
- How to manage uncertainty and complexity are not taught in business schools.
- It merely teaches the concepts with case studies.
- It does not focus on the challenges arising out of rapid growing technology and the challenges involved in running an enterprise.
- Unfortunately, the best talent is going to industry where salaries are lucrative.
- Those who come to academic area are the ones who could not be absorbed in the industry or those who come to this profession by chance or those who chose this career out of passion.
- Insufficient availability of specialised experts and qualified faculty.
- Lack of Industry based specialisations.
- Lower infrastructure.
- Burden with heavy subjects.
- Lack of necessary guidance to the students.
- Lack of updated and industry based syllabus.

- Lack of admissions in Management Research.
- Lack of Inter-disciplinary approach.
- Lack of specified authorities for quality research in management studies.
- Insufficient grants for research.
- The courses remain too theoretical and do not equip students with the right attitudes, skills and knowledge (ASK) required for them to be employable.
- Students are not properly educated either to fit the industry requirements or to be entrepreneurial to start and grow up small and medium companies. Students only get a degree but not the industry-required qualifications.
- Neither the institutions nor the students are clear as to what kind of "product specification" is achieved at the end of the two years of study i.e., the quality of students produced and their ASK levels.
- More than 85 per cent of the students who complete their MBA/PGDM are not industry ready.
- Just as customers would like to know about the specifications and quality before buying any "product", industry would also like to know and be assured of the product specification (Quality) of the Graduates it wants to hire.

13

Indian Institutes of Management

The Indian Institutes of Management (IIMs) are a group of 20 public, autonomous institutes of management education and research in India. They primarily offer postgraduate, doctoral and executive education programmes. The establishment of IIMs was initiated by Jawaharlal Nehru, the first Prime Minister of India, based on the recommendation of the Planning Commission.

IIMs are registered as societies under the Indian Societies Registration Act. Each IIM is autonomous and exercises independent control over its day-to-day operations. However, the administration of all IIMs and the overall strategy of IIMs is overseen by the IIM Council. The IIM Council is headed by India's Minister of Human Resource Development and consists of the chairpersons and directors of all IIMs and senior officials from the Ministry of Human Resource Development of the Government of India.

The Two-year Post Graduate Programme in Management (PGP), offering the Post Graduate Diploma in Management (PGDM), is the flagship programme across all IIMs. These post-graduate diploma programmes are considered the equivalent of regular MBA programmes. Some IIMs also offer a one-year post-graduate diploma programme for graduates with more work experience. Some IIMs offer the Fellow Programme in Management (FPM), a doctoral programme. The fellowship is considered to be equivalent to a Ph.D globally. Most IIMs also offer short-term executive education/EMBA courses and part-time programmes. Some IIMs also offer unique programmes, like IIM-Indore's Five Year Integrated Programme in Management and IIM-Lucknow's Working Managers' Programme of three years.

IIMs (in order of establishment)

Name	Established	Location
Indian Institute of Management, Calcutta	1961	Kolkata
Indian Institute of Management, Ahmedabad	1961	Ahmedabad
Indian Institute of Management, Bengaluru	1973	Bengaluru
Indian Institute of Management, Lucknow	1984	Lucknow
Indian Institute of Management, Kozhikode	1996	Kozhikode
Indian Institute of Management, Indore	1996	Indore
Indian Institute of Management, Shillong	2007	Shillong

Indian Institute of Management, Rohtak	2010	Rohtak
Indian Institute of Management, Ranchi	2010	Ranchi
Indian Institute of Management, Raipur	2010	Raipur
Indian Institute of Management, Tiruchirappalli	2011	Tiruchirappalli
Indian Institute of Management, Kashipur	2011	Kashipur
Indian Institute of Management, Udaipur	2011	Udaipur
Indian Institute of Management, Nagpur	2015	Nagpur
Indian Institute of Management, Visakhapatnam	2015	Visakhapatnam
Indian Institute of Management, Bodh Gaya	2015	Bodh Gaya
Indian Institute of Management, Amritsar	2015	Amritsar
Indian Institute of Management, Sirmaur	2015	Sirmaur district
Indian Institute of Management, Sambalpur	2015	Sambalpur
Indian Institute of Management, Jammu	2016	Jammu

History

After India became independent in 1947, the Planning Commission was entrusted to oversee and direct the development of the nation. India grew rapidly in the 1950s, and in the late 1950s the Commission started facing difficulties in finding suitable managers for the large number of public sector enterprises that were being established in India as a part of its industrial policy. To solve this problem, the Planning Commission in 1959 invited Professor George Robbins of UCLA to help in setting up an All India Institute of Management Studies. Based on his recommendations, the Indian government decided to set up two elite management institutes, named Indian Institutes of Management. Calcutta and Ahmedabad were chosen as the locations for the two new institutes.

The institute at Calcutta was established first, on 13 November 1961, and was named Indian Institute of Management Calcutta or IIM-Kolkata. It was set up in collaboration with the MIT Sloan School of Management, the Government of West Bengal, the Ford Foundation, and Indian industry. The institute at Ahmedabad was established in the following month and was named the Indian Institute of Management Ahmedabad. Like MIT Sloan in the case of IIM-Kolkata, Harvard Business School played an important role in the initial stages of IIM-Ahmedabad.

In 1972, a committee headed by Ravi J. Matthai took note of the success of the two established IIMs and recommended the setting up of two more IIMs. Based on the committee's recommendation, a new IIM, originally intended to cater exclusively to the needs of public sector enterprises, was established in Bengaluru (IIM-Bengaluru) the next year. In 1981, the first IIM Review Committee was convened to examine the progress of the three existing IIMs and to make recommendations. The committee noted that the three IIMs were producing around 400 PGP graduates every year and that they had reached their optimum capacity. It proposed the opening of two more IIMs to meet the rising demand for management professionals. It also recommended expanding the Fellowship programmes, similar to Ph.D programmes, to meet the growing demand for faculty in management schools in India. The fourth IIM, IIM-Lucknow, was established in 1984, based on the committee's recommendation.

Two more IIMs, the fifth and sixth, were established at Kozhikode and Indore in 1996. IIM-Shillong was the seventh IIM to be established, following a 2005 decision by the Government of India, its foundation stone was laid on 1 December 2007; and its first academic session was 2008–09. Since 2007, fourteen new IIMs have been set up, bringing the total number of IIMs to 20, IIM-Jammu being the latest one, starting in 2016.

The Union Cabinet, on 24 January 2017, approved the bill that became the Indian Institutes of Management Act, 2017, which declares IIMs as Institutes of National Importance and enables them to grant degrees and to further make other important changes to the institute. The IIM bill was passed by the Lok Sabha on 28 July 2017 and by the Rajya Sabha on 19 December 2017. After receiving presidential assent, the IIM bill became an Act on 31 December 2017.

Academics

The IIMs mainly offer post-graduate, doctoral, and executive education programmes. Some programmes offered by all IIMs are similar; however, some IIMs offer unique programmes for specialised purposes.

Post-graduate Education

All IIMs offer a two-year full-time Post Graduate Programme in Management (PGP), equivalent to a Master of Business Administration (MBA) degree. The programme is considered the flagship programme of IIMs, and awards the Post Graduate Diploma in Management (PGDM) to successful candidates. This programme is usually structured into six trimesters spread across two years, starting in June and running until April of the second year. The first year coursework generally consists of core courses in various management disciplines, while in the second year students are allowed to select courses from an exhaustive list of electives. The PGP is a general, fully integrated management programme with no specialisation, and typically includes courses in accounting, behavioural science, finance, economics, human-resource management (HRM), management sciences and information technology, marketing, business operations, business mathematics, public policy, statistics and decision analysis, strategy, and general management.

Since 2006, some IIMs have started offering one-year, full-time post-graduate diploma programmes for professionals having approximately 5 years or more of work experience. This programme was necessitated because the normal two-year programme is primarily aimed at new graduates or graduates with less than 4-5 years of work experience. These one-year programmes are general, fully integrated management programmes with no specialisation, and typically include the same courses as offered in a typical two-year MBA programme. These intensive programmes typically require 75 credits or around 750 hours of classroom teaching along with projects and other coursework as in a normal, global two-year MBA programme. (https://en.wikipedia.org/wiki/Indian_Institutes_of_Management - cite_note-62)

Designed as a regular MBA programme, which focuses on using the prior work experience of the students, the one-year MBA is named differently by different IIMs. It is called the Post Graduate Programme for Executives at IIM-Kolkata and IIM-Shillong (PGPEX for short), and at IIM-Ahmedabad and IIM Udaipur (PGPX for short). It is called the Executive Post Graduate Programme (EPGP) at IIM-Bengaluru and IIM-Indore, and the International Programme in Management for Executives (IPMX) at IIM-Lucknow. The exact structure, admission criteria, and other details of these programmes vary. However, all these programmes admit only candidates with approximately 5 or more years of professional experience and usually use a combination of GMAT score, essays, and personal interviews as entry criteria, similar to other globally reputed MBA programmes. The median GMAT score of the batches at IIM-Bengaluru is usually around 710.

IIM-Kolkata offers a Post Graduate Diploma in Computer Aided Management (PGDCM) programme. This course, which was started in 1994, is similar to the regular PGDM programme, but with a special emphasis on information technology and its business applications. It is aimed at creating business professionals who know how to apply information and communication technology (ICT) in business management. Most of the PGDCM coursework is integrated with the regular PGDM framework, and both PGDM and PGDCM are considered as part of the PGP programme. IIM-Ahmedabad and IIM-Lucknow offer a two-year Post Graduate Programme in Agribusiness Management (PGP-ABM) programme. This is essentially an MBA programme with a specialisation in agribusiness. IIM-Ranchi offers a post-graduate programme specialising in human resources, called the Post Graduate Diploma in Human Resource Management (PGDHRM).

Since July 2005, IIM-Lucknow is also offering a three-year Post-Graduate Programme in Management for Working Executives (also known as the Working Managers Programme (WMP)) from its Noida campus, which aims to develop the strong conceptual skills required to manage businesses of the future, to help inculcate leadership and teamwork amongst participants, and to foster the development of change-agents to take leadership roles in the global area.

IIM-Kolkata offers a specialised executive MBA programme called the Post Graduate Programme for Executives for Visionary Leadership in Manufacturing (PGPEX-VLM), jointly with IIT-Kanpur and IIT-Madras. It is a one-year, rigorous programme with a heavy focus on the manufacturing sector.

Doctoral Education

IIMs offer a Fellow Programme in Management (FPM) as a full-time doctoral-level programme in management. This programme is aimed at preparing students for careers in teaching or research in different disciplines of management, as well as for careers outside academics that demand a high degree of investigative and analytical ability. A student, who completes this programme at any IIM, where (s) he is registered as a doctoral scholar, is awarded the title of Fellow of that institute (e.g. Fellow of the Indian Institute of Management - Kolkata). This Fellow Programme is equivalent to the Doctor of Philosophy (Ph.D) degree. Students receiving such a fellowship every year, across all IIMs, work in close association with one another in specific research areas of their choice.

Executive Education

Many IIMs offer executive education-certificate programmes targeted at working professionals. These are often short-term or part-time programmes and are known by various names such as Management Development Programme (MDP), Advanced Master's Programme in Management of Global Enterprises (AMPM), and Executive General Management Programme (EGMP). The certificate programmes at IIMs are not considered as equivalent to an MBA or EMBA. Only the diploma-level programmes are considered as equivalent, depending on whether it is full-time or part-time. Many IIMs—such as IIM-C, IIM-B, IIM-K, IIM-Kashipur, and IIM-Rohtak—have partnered with third-party companies to enable these courses to be provided under a distributed model.

Other Programmes

Some IIMs offer specialised programmes targeted at various management segments. IIM-Ahmedabad offers a six-month, full-time programme called the Armed Forces Programme (AFP) aimed at military personnel. IIM-Ahmedabad and IIM-Bengaluru offer full-time programmes in public management and are called the Post Graduate Programme in Public Management and Policy (PGP-PMP) and Post Graduate Programme in Public Policy Management (PGPPM), respectively. IIM-Bengaluru offers a two-year, part-time programme called the Post-Graduate Programme in Software Enterprise Management (PGPSEM), https://en.wikipedia.org/wiki/ Indian Institutes of Management - cite_note-66, an executive general-management education programme designed for the specific needs of professionals working in the software and information-technology industry. IIM-Indore offers a 5-year Integrated Programme in Management (IPM) that leads to a combined undergraduate-cum-graduate diploma. IIM-Ranchi is the first and only IIM to offer a full-time Post Graduate Diploma in Human Resource Management (PGDHRM) programme.

Admission Process

Different programmes of IIMs follow different admission processes. Admission for residents of India to the flagship two-year PGP programmes at all IIMs is based on the Common Admission Test (CAT). CAT scores are often used as the primary short-listing criteria for admissions. International/ overseas applicants have the option to apply using GMAT scores in lieu of CAT scores. GMAT scores are a prerequisite short-listing criteria used for admission to the one-year full-time programme for experienced executives. Test requirements for doctoral programmes vary. Some IIMs require candidates to make a presentation of a broad research idea or take a Research Aptitude Test (RAT) followed by round of interviews while all are compelled to accept scores on standardised tests such as the CAT, GATE, GMAT, and GRE. The overall profiles of candidates, including past academic and professional accomplishments, are considered for all programmes, along with valid standard test scores. Some programmes require essays and academic or professional recommendations. The final round of admission evaluations involve an interview, before which some IIMs conduct other evaluation processes like written assessment tests and group discussions.

Entrance Exam

The Common Admission Test (CAT) is a management aptitude test conducted by the IIMs primarily as an evaluation tool for admission to their two-year PGP programmes. It is widely considered as one of the most competitive exams in the world, with a success rate of around one in two hundred. Even with the recent addition of new colleges, in 2013 the acceptance rate at IIMs was 1.714 per cent, one of the lowest in the world.

Originally conducted as a paper-and-pencil test given on a particular date all over India, in 2009 CAT began being given as a computer-based assessment operated by Prometric. In 2014, TCS received a 5-year contract to conduct the test. The online test is now given over a period of a few weeks.

In August 2011, the six newer IIMs (Raipur, Rohtak, Ranchi, Udaipur, Trichy and Kashipur) announced that in the coming year they will replace the group-discussion round with a common written analysis test to evaluate communication and comprehension skill. The seven older IIMs did not announce plans to change the admission process.

The admissions for the two-year full-time programme is done by short listing based on GMAT scores in conjunction with candidate profile suitability. This is followed by evaluation of essays and a panel-interview round. The quality of prior work experience and future leadership potential is a critical factor in the selections.

14

Model Curriculum for MBA and PGDM

To improve the quality of management education, AICTE took a major initiative of revising curriculum as a prime reform. A committee under the chairmanship of B. Metri was appointed for Revision of Model Curriculum for MBA and PGDM. The model curriculum emphasised an intensive, flexible core in management education with large number of specialisations and electives including second generation courses. The core courses of MBA/ PGDM programmes are comprised of six key learning outcomes that every employer seeks in management talent. This is a unique future of the model curriculum. This curriculum is designed and developed in such a way that there is a path to suit everyone i.e. full of flexibility and autonomy for department institute to package the courses to position their MBA/PGDM programme. Overall an attempt has been made to connect theory to practice and equip MBA/PGDM students to meet the ever changing needs of the country.

The model curriculum of MBA/PGDM programme emphasissed an intensive flexible management education with 54 credits of core courses and 42 credit electives.

Programme Structure and Credits

The Programme structure and Credits for MBA and PGDM are finalised based on the stakeholders' needs and general structure of the programmes.

Minimum number of classroom contact teaching credits for MBA/ PGDM programme should be 96 credits (one credit equals 10 hours) and field work/ internship should be at 06 credits, thus the minimum number of credits for award of MBA/ PGDM course should be 102 credits. Out of 96 credits, 54 credits are to be allotted for core courses and rest of 42 credits for electives.

MBA Courses	*Number of Credits*
First year (I and II semester)	54 credits of core courses
Second year (III and semesters)	42 credits of electives
Internship/ Field work	06 credits
Total	*102 credits*

PGDM Courses	*Number of Credits*
First year (I, II, III* terms)	54 credits of core courses
Second year (IV, V,VI terms)	42 credits of electives
Internship/ Field work	06 credits
Total	*102 credits*

*University departments/ Institutes based on student interest and faculty resources may offer elective courses in II semester or III trimester also.

Contact hours include work relating to Lecture, Tutorial and Project (LTP), where the academic institution can exercise flexibility to decide course wise requirements.

Core Courses: Core courses of MBA/ PGDM programmes provide a holistic approach to management education, giving students both an overview of the field, and a basis to build, and specialise upon.

These core courses are the strong foundation to establish management knowledge and provide broad multi-disciplined knowledge that can be further studied in depth during the elective phase.

The core courses provide students with more than just practical knowledge, case-based lessons and collaborative learning models, train students to analyse, decide, and lead—rather than merely know— while creating a common student experience that fosters a deep and tenacious community.

A wide range of core courses provide groundwork in the basic management disciplines: accounting, marketing, responsible business, finance, information management system, organisational behavior and human resources, statistics, strategy, and supply chain management. The integrated foundation is important for students because it not only allows them to build upon existing skills, but also to explore career options in a range of industries, and expand their understanding of various business fields. Following table depicts the list of core courses for MBA/ PGDM programmes.

Core Courses for MBA/ PGDM Programmes

Functional Areas	*Core Courses*
Foundation of Management	• Managerial (Micro) Economics • Indian Economy and Policy • Business Communication • Legal and Business Environment (Micro and Macro) • Indian Ethos and Business Ethics
Finance	• Financial Reporting, Statements and Analysis • Corporate Finance • Indian Financial System and Financial Markets
Marketing Management	• Marketing Management • Marketing Research
Operations Management	• Operations Management • Project Management

Management Information System	• Computer Applications for Business
Human Resources Management	• Human Resources Management • Managerial Skills for Effectiveness
Organisational Behaviour	• Organisational Behaviour • Organisation Design
Strategy	• Corporate Strategy • Corporate Social Responsibility and Sustainability • Entrepreneurship
Business Analytics	• Business Statistics and Analytics for Decision making • Quantitative Techniques

Elective Courses

Usually, elective courses fall under at least one of the eight functional areas of business: finance, human resources, organisational behaviour, business analytics, information management, strategy, operations management and marketing. The model curriculum has also identified new and evolving specialisations. These elective courses are: Entrepreneurship, Management of micro and small business management, Retail management, Healthcare management, Social enterprise management, Agribusiness management, Rural management, Education management, Sports management, Infrastructure management, Tourism and Hospitality management. The list of elective courses in functional and non-functional area are portrayed below.

Functional Area	*Elective courses*
Finance	• Investment Analysis and Portfolio Management • Managing Banks and Financial Institutions • Project Appraisal and Finance • Valuation • Financial Markets and Services • Mergers, Acquisitions and Corporate Restructuring • Financial Derivatives • International Finance • Behavioral Finance • Taxation
Marketing Management	• Consumer Behaviour • B2B Marketing • Retail Management • Sales and Distribution Management • Marketing to base of Pyramid Consumers • Integrated Marketing Communications/ Promotion Strategy • Digital and Social Media Marketing • Product and Brand Management • Services Marketing • International Marketing

Operations Management	• Supply Chain and Logistics Management • Quality Toolkit for Managers • Pricing and Revenue Management • Operations Strategy • Sales and Operations Planning • Behavioral Operations Management • Operations Research Applications • Management of Manufacturing Systems • Sourcing Management • Supply Chain Analytics
Human Resources Management	• Manpower Planning, Recruitment, and Selection • Employee Relations • Human Resource Metrics and Analytics • Compensation and Benefits Management • Performance Management Systems • Team Dynamics at Work • Strategic HRM • International HRM • Cross Cultural Management • Understanding Self: Indian Perspective
Organisational Behaviour	• Organisational Change and Development • Leadership
Strategy	• Strategic Management of Services • Competing in Global Markets • Dynamics of Framing and Executing Strategy • Entrepreneurship in Practice • Foundations of Strategy Consulting • Strategic Leadership • Designing and Configuring Business Models • Corporate Governance
Management Information System	• Data Mining for Business Decisions • Managing Software Projects • Managing Digital Innovation and Transformation • IT Consulting • E-Commerce and Digital Markets • Strategic Management of IT • Managing Digital Platforms
Business Analytics	• Data Visualisation for Managers • Business Forecasting • Data Science using R • Data Mining • Marketing Analytics
Non-Functional Area	• Elective Courses

Entrepreneurship	• Technology Appreciation and Intellectual Property Rights • Innovation Technology Management • Indian Models in Entrepreneurship • Social Entrepreneurship • Venture Valuation and Accounting • Entrepreneurial Marketing • Entrepreneurship Lab
International Business	• Design and Change in Organisations • Planning, Structuring, and Financing Small Business • Business Plan Preparation for Small Business • Marketing for Small Business • Finance and Accounting for Small Business
Retail Management	• Logistic and Supply Chain Aspects in Retail Management • Retail Brand Management • Retail Consumer Behaviour • E–retailing
Other possible Specialisations/ Electives in Emerging Areas	• Infrastructure Management, Tourism and Hospitality Management, Health Care • Management, Social Enterprise Management, Agri-Business Management, • Educational Institutions Management, Sports Management, Management of Rural • Business.

Note: Apart from these electives, students can choose Global Virtual Teams (GVT) as Course of Independent Study (CIS) or Study Abroad Project/Experiential/Live Project in place of elective courses.

Students in MBA programmes can define what areas of study would like to pursue, or even take some courses from other departments of university based on their educational background. These elective courses are taught through the combination of readings, lectures, cases, group presentations, experiential exercises and class discussion, which allow entering MBA/ PGDM students to determine their own leadership strengths and limitations, and to develop a plan for improving their strengths and overcoming their limitations.

Other Possible Specialisations in Emerging Areas

The application of business management skills and competencies have found to be relevant in various emerging business areas, providing wide spread employment and entrepreneurship opportunities to the graduates. The business schools/ institutions may offer specially designed electives to strengthen the competencies of the students and meeting the requirements of enterprises. We outline these courses as; Infrastructure Management, Tourism and hospitality Management, Health care Management, Social enterprise management, Agri-business management, Educational Institutions Management, Sports Management, Management of Rural Business.

Alternative Study Credit Activities

Today, there is a need to prepare MBA/ PGDM students for a VUCA (Volatile Uncertain, Complex and Ambiguous) world. Business models are being redefined, and the lines between careers, industries and geographical boundaries are constantly being redrawn. To stay relevant, MBA/ PGDM students must go beyond the boundaries of their campus.

The future very much rests on how current and future leaders are being prepared, both inside and outside of the classroom by MBA/ PGDM programmes. Higher education today is no longer confined to the classroom alone. The classroom is now less a place for knowledge transmission than a platform for development i.e. to apply acquired information to debates and discussions, drive inquisitiveness as well as develop causal thinking and analytical prowess.

Employers expect graduates to be work-ready from day one and are increasingly focused on applicants' verifiable skills. Thus, non-classroom non-traditional sources of learning have a critical role to play. It is about the context and environment for learning and development. Students should be taken outside the walls of the campus to learn at various locations around the city, and the world, in order to put lessons into a larger context. Also, it helps the students to develop communication and networking skills to obtain the information they need, and then employ their own analysis, judgment and moral compass to make the right decisions.

Business schools are much more integral part of their surrounding community. Students should work on projects that strengthen local organisations, government, businesses and the society.

Engagement is an important aspect of producing management education that is responsible and accountable. To meet the demand for work-ready graduates, experiential learning is an essential curriculum component.

Apart from core and elective courses, the following vital programmes (with appropriate credits) engage and empower students by allowing them to discuss, debate and solve real business challenges are to be considered as alternatives for the core and elective courses for MBA/PGDM programme:

1. Outbound Experiential Learning Programmes
2. Communication Through Theatre Techniques
3. Course of Independent Study
4. MOOC Courses
5. NSE and other similar Certification Programmes
6. Social Sensitisation Projects
7. Community Development Projects
8. Rural Innovation Projects
9. Consulting Projects

10. Industry or Academic Internships
11. Field/Live Projects
12. Global Virtual Team Project
13. Study Abroad Programme
14. Student Exchange Programmes

Through above activities students demonstrate their ability to apply learned skills and also students push boundaries and propose and explore much needed solutions across disciplines and cultures. Every institute is expected to conduct special workshops, business thought leadership series, resume writing and career development counselling, to improve the personality of students and make them confident to face the employment process.

15

Distance Courses

Distance education is very popular among those who wish to obtain Management Education qualification, particularly the employed persons in different areas. Some of such persons are:

- Working professionals, who want to take their careers to the next level and want to pursue MBA degree course but do not have time to attend the regular classes because they are doing full time job.
- House wives, who want to continue their study but cannot go to colleges to attend the lectures.
- Fresh graduates, who wish to join job but also want to continue their higher studies.
- Those who want to make their career in the field of business management.

Additionally more than 5,00,000 students complete MBA degree programme each year and the number is increasing each passing year.

MBA is the only degree programme popularity of which is increasing year by year. MBA degree from a reputed university can open up several doors for one's career. One can pick up a specialisation of their choice out of the tons of specialisation available.

There are hundreds of MBA colleges offering Distance MBA in India. But there are only very few top distance management colleges that offer good value. Best Distance MBA colleges have a few common features like recognition by UGC, good brand name, updated curriculum and affordable fee.

Some Top Distance Education MBA Colleges

MBAUniverse.com experts analysed over hundred distance MBA colleges and programmes and selected the best Distance MBA University and Colleges in India. The list is

1. NMIMS Global Access School for Continuing Education
2. Symbiosis Centre for Distance Education
3. IMT Centre for Distance Learning
4. Indira Gandhi National Open University
5. Sikkim Manipal University

6. Welingkar Institute of Management
7. Amity University
8. Annamalai University

www.gyanunlimited.com listed sixty-five universities, colleges, institutions that offer managementcourses through Distance Education, Correspondence and Open Learning.

www.distnaceeducation360.com identified the following ten top Distance Education Institutes in India for MBA/PGDM:

1. Institute of Management Studies
2. Symbiosis Centre for Distance Learning
3. Indira Gandhi National Open University
4. ICFAI University
5. Sikkim Manipal University
6. Annamalai University
7. Narsee Monjee Institute of Management Studies
8. Prin LN Weligkar Institute of Management
9. Amity University
10. Lovely Professional University

MBA from IGNOU

IGNOU is one of the largest providers of Distance Education in the world. The university was established by the Government of India and is an autonomous institution under it. MBA programme is approved by UGC and AICTE. This makes it acceptable anywhere in India.

Successful completion of a specific combination of courses would lead to:

- Master of Business Administration (MBA), or
- Post Graduate Diploma in Human Resource Management (PGDHRM), or
- Post Graduate Diploma in Financial Management (PGDFM), or
- Post Graduate Diploma in Operations Management (PGDGM), or
- Post Graduate Diploma in Marketing Management (PGDMM), or
- Post Graduate Diploma in Financial Markets Practice (PGDFMP)

Master of Business Administration (MBA)

The MBA Programme consists of 21 courses in all. These comprise of:

- All the courses from MSl to MS-09 and MS-ll
- Five courses from any one of the specialisation streams
- Compulsory courses (MS-l0, MS-9l, MS-95) and any one elective course out of MS-92/93/94/96/97
- Project course (MS-l00) equivalent to 2 courses.

IGNOU follows a modular approach in its programme offering viz. if a student takes admission into MBA and for some reason or the other is not able to complete all the courses/ he is provided with exit point. If s/he completes 6 courses in a particular specialisation along with the compulsory basic course s/he would be awarded Post Graduate Diploma in that particular specialisation.

Post-graduate Diploma in Management

Post Diploma in Management comprises 11 courses Programme

Programme	*Course Code*	*Course Title*
Post Graduate Diploma in Management (PGDMM)	MS-l	Management Functions and behaviour
	MS-2	Mânagement of Human Behaviour
	MS-3	Economic and Social Environment
	MS-4	Accounting and Finance for Managers
	MS-5	Management of Machines and Minerals
	MS-6	Marketing for Managers
	MS-7	Information Systems for Managers
	MS-8	Quantitative Analysis for Managerial Applications
	MS-9	Managerial Economics
	MS-l0	Organisational Design and Development and Change
	Ms-l1	Strategic Management

Specialisation Programmes

Programme P G Diploma in	*Course Code*	*Course Title*
Human Resource Management (PGDHRM)	MS-21	Social Processes and Behavioural Issues
	MS-22	Human Resource Development
	MS-23	Human Resource Planning
	MS-24	Employment Relations
	MS-ZS	Managing Change in Organisations
	MS-26	Organisational Dynamics
	MS-27	Wage and Salary Administration
	MS-28	Labour Laws
	MS-29	International Human Resource Management
Financial Management (PGDFM)	MS-41	Working Capital Management
	MS_42	Capital Investment and Financing Decisions
	MS-43	Management Control Systems
	MS-44	Security Analysis and Portfolio Management
	MS-45	International Financial Management
	MS-46	Management of Financial Services

Operations Management (PGDOM)	MS-51	Operations Research
	MS-52	Project Management
	MS-53	Production/Operation Management
	MS-54	Management Information Systems
	MS-55	Logistics and Supply Chain Management
	MS-56	Materials Management
	MS-57	Maintenance Management
	Ms-58	Management of R&D and Innovation
Marketing Management (PGDMM)	MS_61	Consumer Behaviour
	MS-62	Sales Management
	MS-63	Product Management
	MS-64	International Marketing
	MS_65	Marketing of Services
	MS-66	Marketing Research
	MS-68	Management of Marketing Communication and Advertising
	MS-611	Rural Marketing
	MS-612	Retail Marketing
Financial Markets Practice (PGD-FMP)	MFP-1	Equity Markets
	MFP-2	Equity Derivatives
	MFP-3	Commodity Markets
	MFP-4	Currency and Debt Markets
	MFP-5	Professionals in Financial Markets Practice

16

Entrepreneurial Intention

The entrepreneurial intention among the management graduates had been rising in the recent years and it became national agenda of Indian policy makers, educationist and development agencies. At the same time the percentage of graduates as job creators has reduced and the job seekers have increased. Management Institutes provide management skills, entrepreneurial qualities and networking opportunities to enable graduate to start and run the business effectively. At the same time there are so many other factors, which play a lead role in deciding the entrepreneurial intention of the graduates in addition to the personal, social and economic factors.

G. Manoja and P.G. Arul of the Department of International Business of Pondicherry University carried out a study by taking into consideration the above three factors as to how influence the management graduate in deciding their option to become job-seekers or job generators.

Motivational Factors

Entrepreneurial motivation is one of the major predictors of entrepreneurial behaviour, therefore, special consideration should be given to explore the causes behind students' entrepreneurial intention. From the perspective of a potential entrepreneurial, like university student's entrepreneurship being with the motivations, but whether the motivations are transformed into reality or not depends on many factors.

Personal Factors: Factors like risk taking, achievement, job security, environment to start business, first to achieve are considered as motivating factors., Various factors such as 'to lead other people', 'implementing ideas' 'to be own boss' 'non-business education and personal challenges in life lead to entrepreneurial motivation. Attitude, perceived behavior control and norms act as factors for entrepreneurial intention. Perceived desirability and perceived feasibility have a positive impact on entrepreneurial intention.

Social Factors: Entrepreneurial intention is also perceived by relatives, parents, colleagues and friends as an important factor to have certain perceptions and behaviors.

Economic Factors: Economic factors like legal rules support of the government act as an important factor for entrepreneurial intention. Socio-environment factors act as supporting as well as hindering factors for entrepreneurial intention.

Analysis of Factors

The motivating factors to become an entrepreneur factors and various factors concerning the personal, social and environment factor to become an entrepreneur.

Among the three factors that make the students as entrepreneurs after completion of their course, personal factors stand first and to be more specific the attributes like ‘to be one’s own boss’ ‘entrepreneurial goals’ gain more weight. Seconds stands the social factors and lastly comes the economic factors, which clearly indicate that personal factors are the main motivating force for a student to become an entrepreneur.

17
Accreditation

Accreditation, for an educational institution, is a process of validation in which colleges, universities and other institutions of higher learning are evaluated. It is a ratification of the quality of education provided by the institution. An institute can seek certification from mandatory and other organisations.

Accreditation is considered a must for various reasons. Firstly, it is a self-evaluation tool for the institution to understand and continuously improve upon its deliverables. Leading international professional accrediting organisations make it mandatory to provide a self-evaluation report which will be the initial process to be eligible for the institution to be considered for accreditation. Self-evaluation report need to be update to prove a continuous improvement during the process and final accreditation. Secondly, it is a means for potential candidates to find the right B-School. Since accreditation endorses the minimum quality compliance, it helps students choose the right and relevant institution. The level and accrediting body will help potential students to map the institution they would like to be trained to make excel in their chosen career. Thirdly, it is the choice of destination for employers in seeking new talent. Accreditation helps corporate identity the best-in-class institutions and empanel them for talent acquisition.

Benefits of Accreditation

B-Schools offering accredited management education prepare students for leadership roles in a variety of business settings. An MBA is unlike any other Master's programme in the sense that instead of focusing on a particular specialisation, it exposes students to different areas of business such as finance, accounting, marketing, human resources, operations management, etc.

But why is accreditation so important for B-Schools? What benefits does it offer to institutions, graduates, and employers?

The biggest benefit of an accreditation is that it is a stamp of approval for the quality of education being imparted at an institution from a recognised third-party organisation. Not only is it a measure of a school's academic standards and teaching practices, but also its student services, quality of faculty etc.

For potential students, accreditation provides an assurance of the quality of business education they will receive. It ensures that students will be rewarded for the time and money, they are committing to by enrolling in a particular MBA programme.

A systematic and standardised review process that is involved in granting and maintaining accreditation also allows schools to identify areas of strengths, weaknesses, and opportunities and work on them.

Accreditation encourages institutions to look for new, innovative, and modern methods of pedagogy, which ultimately lead to enhanced educational experience for students and consequently higher patronage.

Accreditation also helps an institution gain more visibility, international credibility, and enhanced status. Since they have to submit to rigorous standards of quality to receive and maintain accreditation, it puts them on the path to continuous self-improvement.

As far as employers are concerned, accreditation is an undeniable proof that the graduates, they are about to hire, have received the finest quality and highly relevant business education.

NAAC and NBA

There are two central bodies involved in accreditation: NAAC and NBA. The NAAC was setup in 1994 by the UGC for institutional accreditation through a combination of internal and external quality assessment.

The NBA was originally constituted in 1994 to assess the qualitative competence of the educational institutions from Diploma level to Postgraduate level in Engineering and Technology, Management, Pharmacy, Architecture, and related discipline. The NBA in its present form, has come into existence as an autonomous body with effect from January 2010, with objective of assurance of quality and relevance of the technical education through the mechanisms of accreditation of programmes offered by technical institutions.

Main objectives of the NBA are to

a) assess and grade colleges and/or institutions of technical and professional education, the courses and programmes offered by them, their various units, faculty, departments etc.,
b) stimulate the academic environment and quality of teaching and research in these institutions,
c) contribute to the sphere of knowledge in its discipline,
d) motivate colleges and/or institutions of technical and professional education for research, and adopt teaching practices that groom their students for the innovation and development of leadership qualities,
e) encourage innovation, self-evaluation and accountability in higher education,

f) promote necessary changes, innovation and reforms in all aspects of the working of the colleges/ institutions of technical and professional education for the above purpose, and
g) help institutions to realise their academic objectives.

NBA Committees for Accreditation

Evaluation and Accreditation Committee (EAC)

The EAC is constituted for each discipline (Engineering and Technology / Management/Pharmacy/ Architecture) to review the evaluation team reports and submit its recommendations on accreditation to the EC. The composition of the EAC is as follows.

1. The chairman of the EAC, appointed by the EC, is an eminent academician from academia or a distinguished professional from industries/R&D organisations/professional bodies.
2. Three experts from the respective discipline (with different specialisations).
3. One expert from industries/R&D organisations.
4. One representative from professional bodies.
5. One representative of the NBA nominated by the Member Secretary of the NBA.

Appellate Committee (AC)

The grievances and redressal of the institution received by the NBA, on the accreditation of the programmes shall be addressed by the Appellate Committee. The composition of the AC is as follows:

1. The Chairman of the AC, appointed by the EC, shall be an eminent academician from academia or a distinguished professional from industries/R&D organisations/professional bodies.
2. One expert (preferably from engineering) from academia.
3. One representative from industries/R&D organisations.
4. One representative from professional bodies.
5. One legal representative nominated by the Member Secretary of the NBA.

Accreditation Policy

The following general policies are the guiding principles for the accreditation of Business Schools:

1. Educational institutions are accredited at present.
2. Business schools to be accredited should be those which have been formally approved by the appropriate designated authority or authorities, as the case may be.

3. Business schools which have produced postgraduates for at least two academic years will be considered for full accreditation and, provisional accreditation, as the case may be.
4. Business schools will be considered for assessment and accreditation only at the written request of the educational institution and after agreeing to abide by the NBA's accreditation manual, rules, regulations and notification issued from time to time.
5. Accreditation will normally be granted for a specific term of up to a maximum of five academic years. Provisional accreditation may also be granted to new business schools (not matured for full accreditation).
6. After accreditation, the institutions are expected to submit their annual self-assessment report to eNBA online. If any aspect of the programme is found to be sufficiently unsatisfactory and/or does not comply with norms, the NBA reserves the right to revoke the accreditation. If necessary, the NBA may appoint a maximum of two members to form an Evaluation Team to act as mentors at the request of institution. The mentor(s) may visit the educational institution at its request for mentoring purposes and provide a report to the NBA on their findings for each visit. The educational institution will bear the expenses of the visit and pay honorarium to the mentors as prescribed by the NBA.
7. Accreditation is based on satisfying the minimum standards.
8. All correspondence between the educational institution and the NBA vis-à-vis accreditation process is confidential and may not be revealed to any unauthorised persons under any circumstances, except with written permission from the concerned educational institution.
9. A three day onsite visit shall be a part of the accreditation process. An evaluation team appointed by the NBA will carry out the evaluation of the business school. The evaluation team consists of evaluators and is headed by a chairperson. The institute shall propose such set of dates for visit when the regular classes and all academic activities are on.
10. The final decision made by the NBA will be communicated to the educational institution together with comments which portray strengths, weaknesses and scope for improvement. In the event that a business school is not accredited, reasons for the decision will also be given. If accreditation is denied and if the educational institution wishes, it may appeal against the decision to the Appellate Committee (AC).
11. The educational institution shall bear the cost of accreditation, as per the fee prescribed by the NBA.

Global Accreditation

As internationalisation of higher education gains ground in India, leading B-Schools are scrambling for global accreditations to boost their brand name, improve rankings and enhance collaborations in academics and research.

Indian schools are opting for three kinds of accreditations: the UK's Association of MBAs (AMBA), the European Quality Improvement System (EQUIS) and the American AACSB (Association to Advance Collegiate Schools of Business). While EQUIS and AACSB accredit overall performance of a management school, AMBA accredits individual programmes. "We don't want to remain just a good B-School in India. The aim is to have same credentials globally and for that, global accreditation is a must" B P Abraham, Dean Academics at the Indian Institute of Management Kolkata (IIM-C) said in an interview.

IIM-C is the only Indian school to have AMBA, EQUIS and AACSB accreditations, known in the management education world as "triple crown".

Abraham said a school benefits from such accreditation in three ways. First, it helps the school get foreign students, thus improving diversity on the campus; second, it attracts the best schools in the world to have collaborations and third, the brand profile of a school goes up globally. For example, IIM-C has now partnerships with 91 top B-Schools from across the globe and most of them have global accreditations.

Not just IIM-C, IIMs at Ahmedabad, Bengaluru, Indore, Lucknow, Kozhikode, Management Development Institute in Gurugram; International Management Institute (IMI) in New Delhi; Institute of Management Technology (IMT) Ghaziabad; TA Pai Management Institute (TAPMI), Manipal; SP Jain Institute of Management and Research (SPJIMR), Mumbai; and Xavier School of Management (XLRI), Jamshedpur, were among a growing number of top B-Schools who have bagged one or more international accreditations. Besides, nearly two dozen other schools in India are in the process of bagging such accreditation.

The Indian School of Business (ISB) Hyderabad won EQUIS accreditation and coveted AACSB accreditation. The school said the AACSB and EQUIS authorities evaluated its quality measures. The school said such bodies evaluate the institution's focus on internationalisation and ethics, its connections with the corporate world, and how it balances between academic and managerial relevance.

B-School authorities said Indian schools lag behind in global rankings largely due to their poor internationalisation-both in terms of students, faculties and joint research. With global accreditation gaining currency in the country, the Indian schools may see a marked improvement in global league tables.

AACSB's accreditation standards are designed to help schools discover-and deliver on-their differentiated mission, so they can foster meaningful change through engagement, innovation, and impact. Among thousands of B-Schools globally, only 799 schools from 53 countries have AACSB accreditation.

According to AACSB, it looks at "excellence in areas relating to strategic management and innovation; student, faculty, and staff as active participants; learning and teaching; and academic and professional engagement" among other factors.

Accreditation of Faculty

The faculty is academically qualified, but one also looks at their professional qualification in different academic components to have overall quality standards. The accreditation principle lies on the platform that a part from degree, multiple catagories of academic activities and outcomes that may support qualification including professional activity, professional development, intellectual contribution, academic contribution, etc. are the key to demonstrate the credentials as quality faculty.

With the accreditation of institutes and programmes, there is also a strong need of faculty accreditation at a larger level, with reputable councils and competent authority on higher education taking the initiative of accreditating management faculty to establish and certify as a certified teacher in the field of management education.

There are several surveys which speak about Ranking of B-School based on certain parameters like infrastructure, knowledge delivery, corporate interface, placements, and pedagogy approach a part from intellectual generation, paper publication, paper presentation, book published and the like. Even audits are conducted from time to time to verify the standards maintained in these area. The most crucial area like "Accreditation of Faculty" is never brought to the table of discussion nor figures in any of the process or audit. If we look at the surveys and rankings of B-Schools, there has not been a subject of "Accreditation of the Faculty".

In India we have currently many business schools producing over 2-3 lakhs management graduates every year and this analysis makes us realise the huge number of management faculty, who are involved in teaching in these institutions and who are the actual facilitators of management education. They become a very crucial section of the community when an institution is accredited, but then what really matters is their recognition as management faculty. Is there a way by which they are formally recognised for their professional excellence and get certified for their professional credentials? Academic grades are given due credit and because of that, they are in the process of imparting management education, per se. When it comes to the question of professional excellence, contribution and quality delivery, there should be an honor of recognition, opportunity for reflection and award for their contributions in different academic domains. This is where researchers felt that there is a need, that some more organisations like AIMA or similar competent authority in Higher Education should take the initiative to recognise management faculty by adopting a procedure and analysing them on certain parameters which evaluates them for their expertise as management teachers, thus, recognising and confirming Professional Status - a stamp for excellence and quality.

When we say Faculty Accreditation, we necessarily mean:

1. Exceeding stated standards of quality performance in academics and related academic areas
2. Production of Intellectual contributions and Professional Development
3. The need for maintaining Academic Qualification and also the Professional Qualification, and
4. On entering at very senior leadership roles and higher levels in academics (Dean/ Director), an Accredited teacher on the resume will stand out more to employer than one of the questionable integrity.

Professor M.M. Bagali of Jain University CMS Business School developed a model for Faculty Accreditation. Faculty for accreditation will be judged in each of the four areas:

1. Teaching
2. Discovery
3. Knowledge integration
4. Service.

There are the areas where faculty can contribute significantly and demonstrate superior and differentiating work.

All those faculty/teachers, who are into teaching in management schools with Ph.D from a recognised university, are eligible for the Professional Accreditation Teacher (PAT) award. Further, a full time teaching experience at PG level with 5 years should be mandatory. The experience in teaching at PG level should be considered equal to the corporate experience at middle management level. SOP-Statement of Purpose of getting PAT may be justified.

Accreditation, for an educational institution, is a process of validation in which colleges, universities and other institutions of higher learning are evaluated. It is a ratification of the quality of education being provided as the institution fulfills its identified mission. An institute can seek certification from a few mandatory and other organisations. For Business Schools, the golden standard of accreditation is AACSB (Association of Advanced Collegiate Schools of Business). EQUIS and AMBA are the other two world-renowned authorising establishments.

International accreditations broaden the thinking of a B-School through associations with world class institutions, thus improving the overall outcomes. If the accreditation is attained from leading and influential accreditation associations, the value will be manifold, impacting all stakeholders.

Accreditation is considered a must for various reasons. Firstly, it is a self-evaluation tool for the institution to understand and continuously improve upon its deliverables. Leading international professional accrediting organisations make it mandatory to provide a self-evaluation report which will be the initial process to be eligible for the Institution to be considered for accreditation. Self-Evaluation Reports (SER) need to be updated to prove a continuous improvement during the process and final accreditation. Secondly, it is a means for potential candidates to find the right B-School: Since accreditation endorses the minimum quality compliance, it helps students choose the right and relevant Institution. The level and the accrediting body will help potential students to map the institution they would like to be trained to make excel in their chosen career. Thirdly, it is the choice of destination for employers in seeking new talent: Accreditation helps corporate identify the best-in-class Institutions and empanel them for talent acquisition.

International Accreditation

As Indian B-Schools aspire to become truly global in various aspects – student intake, quality of education, placements and participation in international ranking – more and more of them are looking for international accreditation.

Merely an approval by AICTE or affiliation to a university/AIU, no longer establishes the quality of a business management programme. Even an accreditation by NAAC no longer enhances reputation of these programmes.

Among the 15,000 plan B-Schools in the world roughly 4,000 are in India. 'However, less than 0.25 per cent of Indian B-Schools have received any of prestigious international accreditation.

While international accreditations are a costly affair, both in terms of financial investment and resource mobilisation in addition to tedious and time-taking process: they certainly offer a whole lot of tangible and intangible benefits – both in short and long terms. These internationally accredited institutions become more attractive to global students, faculty and recruiters alike and stand with higher ability to create a price differentiation. On the other hand it also helps in creating diversity of students as well as faculty. Such international accreditation gives an advantage of international recognition, status and exposure.

All these accreditations are based on assessment and verifications of several parameters, including rigour in admissions process, learning expectations and assurance, faculty quality, course curriculum, infrastructure, international interface, ethics, diversity, innovation, placements, among others it serves the B-Schools by informing them of their strengths and weakness vis-a-vis their global pears.

There are three international accrediting organisations:

- The Association of Advance Collegiate Schools of Business (AACSB)
- The Association of MBAs (AMBA)
- The European Quality Improvement System (EQUIS)

While each of these uses different systems on which to base their assessments of schools, all are highly evolved and provide high benchmarks for acceptance.

AACSB

The US-based Association to Advance Collegiate Schools of Business (AACSB) was established in 1916 as a membership's organisation for business schools. In 1919 the first AACSB Accreditation standards were adopted with the primary objective of improving collegiate business education. Today the AACSB Accreditation Standards are used as the basis to evaluate a business school's missions, operations, faculty qualifications and contributions, programmes and other critical areas. AACSB's accreditation standards drive impact, innovation and engagement with students, employers and various stakeholders. The standards are rigorous, relevant and benchmarks of quality.

Currently, the following Indian Business Schools are accredited by AACSB.

1. IIM, Kolkata
2. ISB, Hyderabad
3. T.A.Pai Management, Manipal

One should remember that there are several B-Schools which are members of AACSB, but have not received accreditation.

AMBA

The Association of MBAs is one of the major accreditation bodies for postgraduate business education and was established in 1967. The London based group positions itself as the world's impartial authority on postgraduate management education.

The AMBA system judges the quality of business school's strategy, mission, faculty, students, curriculum and assessment. For example, to be accepted as an AMBA accredited school's programme must have at least three years of work experience and three quarters of a business school's faculty must have Masters or Doctoral degree in a relevant discipline. It differs from AACSB and EQUIS as it accredits a school's portfolio of postgraduate business programme rather than the entire business school.

To date AMBA has accredited programmes at 240 business schools in over 70 countries. Its process of accrediting an MBA programme includes reviewing compliance with over 100 criteria most of them qualitative rather than quantitative. The criteria falls into seven dimensions — history and development of the institute; facilities and libraries; teaching faculty; teachings standards and research track records; programme administration; career and cohort size; curriculum contents; programme mode and duration and learning outcomes.

Some of the key AMBA criteria for the accreditation of an MBA programme include

- All admitted students should have at least three years of full time post-graduation work experience upon the start of the MBA course.
- A school should have a track record of at least three years of graduating MBA students before it can be accredited.
- An MBA programme should have a cohort size of atleast 20 student
- Atleast 50 per cent of the faculty of an MBA programme are normally expected to have Ph.D degree.
- A full time MBA curriculum should contain no less than 500 contact hours and a distance learning MBA programme should have no less than 120 contact hours.

The following business school in India are AMBA accredited:

1. IIM-Kolkata
2. IIM-Kozhikode
3. IIM-Lucknow
4. International Management Institute, Delhi
5. Management Development Institute Gurugram
6. S.P Jain Institute of Management and Research, Mumbai
7. Great Laker Institute of Management, Chennai

EQUIS

EQUIS (managed by the Brussels – based European Foundation for Management Development) is one of the major international systems of quality assessment, improvement and accreditation for business schools that provide courses in management and business administration. EQUIS evaluates a business school's governance, strategy, programmes, students, faculty, research and development, executive education, contribution to the community, resources and administrates internationalisation and corporate connections. The fundamental objective of EQUIS is to raise the standard of management education world-wide. EQUIS attaches importance to the creation of an effective learning environment that favours the development of students' managerial and entrepreneurial skills and fosters their sense of global responsibility. It also looks for innovation in all respects, including programme design and pedagogy.

Only two school in India accredited by EQUIS:

1. IIM, Ahmedabad
2. IIM, Bengaluru

SAQS

The Association of Management Development Institutions in South Asia based one provides SAQS (South Asia Quality Assurance Systems) accreditation which involves mentoring, self-assessment documentation, peer review and apex committee evaluation.

In India twelve institutes have received SAQS accreditation. Some of such ones are:

1. Management Development Institute, Gurugram
2. International Management Institute, New Delhi
3. Institute of Management Technology, Ghaziabad

ACBSP

Accreditation Council for Business Schools and Programmes (ACBSP) was established to accredit business schools with emphasis on teaching and learning. Currently ACBSP accredits nearly 8000 programmes at over 1200 campuses across the World. However, ACBSP accreditation is widely seen as less stringent than of other accreditation bodies such as AACSB, EQUES and AMBA. Currently, some programmes of core Business schools in India are accredited by AABSP. Some examples are:

1. Amity University, Noida
2. Lovely Professional University, Punjab
3. Apeejay School of Management, New Delhi

18

Industry Interface

Industry interface is perhaps the most critical differentiator for B-Schools worldwide. It also has a strong bearing on a school's intellectual capital. In India, the level of interface is very low and there are some misconceptions, too. Public relations work done for placing students, such as organising guest lectures and seminars are often the activity that B-Schools do in the name of industry interface.

The critical indicators of the level of industry interface are the number of joint research projects taken up with industry, the number of field cases authored by faculty, the number of live cases that students take up with industry, the number of open management development programmes (MDPs) conducted, the number of consulting projects taken up by faculty and the revenue generated from them, and the frequency of revamping the curriculum and its relevance. Barring a few institutes, all Indian B-Schools measure poorly against these parameters.

B-Schools need to revamp their organisational structure, systems and processes for effective interaction with industry.

According to Premchand Palety, Director of Centre for Forecasting and Research in New Delhi expresses how this should be accomplished.

Industry Representation

The starting point of good industry interface is the composition of the governing board of the institute, which in my view should have at least 30 per cent of members from industry. In addition to this, industry representation is necessary in the academic council of every area/specialisation of the institute to review the curriculum and plan other activities every year. The industry representative should belong to the industry that recruits students from the institute in that particular area. The representative should be active in day-to-day activities of his/her organisation and not some retired official looking for a pastime.

Their feedback in designing curriculum and shaping the students is very important. The governing board should meet every quarter and the area meeting to review curriculum and the other relevant activities should be held at least once a year. The key decisions taken in every meeting should be documented and the percentage of those decisions implemented should also be recorded.

Corporate Relations Officer

The institute should also have a corporate relations officer, who is responsible for maintaining interaction with industry. This person should be a specialist in his profession and should not be a faculty member, who often does a bad job balancing academic work with the added responsibility.

All faculty members must be active in at least one of the activities that connect them to industry which is consultancy, research projects and training. The institute should aspire to have at least half of its revenue from these activities. For this, faculty members should be given enough space and resources. Teaching load should not be more than four courses in a year. Independent cabins, access to reputed national and international journals, sufficient funds to interact with industry are important inputs needed to enable faculty to build their competencies and reach out to industry.

Field Cases

The output of faculty should be measured in terms of cases developed, joint research projects undertaken, consultancy assignments and MDPs conducted. The faculty should author cases by interacting with industry. As of now, most of the cases written by Indian B-School faculty are armchair efforts and not field cases. Institutes should constantly come up with new learning that can be gain fully adopted by industry. MDPs are meant to be a means to disseminate new learning created in institutes among professionals from industry. Unfortunately, many MDPs, especially the in-company programmes, are just refresher courses that are conducted more as a formality to meet the training budgets of industry, and there are unethical practices associated with them. I have come across such programmes where the participants feel it's just a means to get away from routine work and there is hardly any serious learning.

Some B-Schools are known for their "public relation skills" in getting such assignments. Public sector companies are more comfortable offloading their training budgets on government-aided B-Schools irrespective of the competence ofthe faculty. Participation in open programmes, by contrast, is a measure of the quality of the faculty conducting the programme. As participation is not mandatory and is open to all, only persons who feel that they will learn something attend such programmes.

Seminars, workshops, guest lectures and hiring visiting faculty from industry have become means to "network" with industry to ensure good placements rather than learning. Visiting faculty from industry should be hired only for highly specialised electives. They should be practicing managers at the senior level. Besides, summer internship of eight weeks as is the usual practice, students should also take up live cases with industry under the guidance of faculty.

Good interface with industry ensures that faculty members are keeping pace with the fast changing scenario of industry which is mirrored in the knowledge and skills of students, who don't need much training on being hired.

19
Globalisation Impact

The term 'globalisation' means integration of economies and societies through cross country flows of information, ideas, technologies, goods, services, capital, finance and people. Cross border integration can have several dimensions – cultural, social, political and economic.

Globalisation is a feature of changing world. It is no more a recent phenomenon in the world and since India is major player of twenty first century we are facing its socio-economic impacts. Initial enthusiasm for globalisation as a beneficial set of processes has yielded to an understanding that the phenomenon is largely associated with increasing social inequality within and between countries as well as instability and conflict.

Globalisation is impacting the institutional framework in both developing and industrial countries. It is changing the way in which governments perceive their role in the society. It has also far reaching implications for socio economic development and educational systems of countries all over the world.

Knowledge is the driving force in the rapidly changing globalised economy and society. Quantity and quality of specialised human resources determine their competence in the global market. Emergence of knowledge as driving factor results in both challenges and opportunities. It is well known that the growth of the global economy has increased opportunities for those countries with good levels of education.

Globalisation has a multi-dimensional impact on the system of education. It promotes new tools and techniques in this area like E-learning, Flexible learning, Distance Education Programmes and Overseas training. Globalisation will mean many different things for education. In the near future, "it will mean a more competitive and deregulated educational system modelled after free market but with more pressure on it to assure that the next generation of workers are prepared for some amorphous 'job market of 21st century'.

The benefits of globalisation accrue to the countries with highly skilled human capital and it is a curse for the countries without such specialised human capital. Developing and transition countries are further challenged in a highly competitive world economy because their higher education systems are not adequately developed for the creation and use of knowledge. Converting the challenges into opportunities depend on the rapidity at which they adapt to the changing environment.

Globalisation is expected to have a positive influence on the volume, quality and spread of knowledge through increased interaction among the various states.

Today, our educational system is strong enough but Central and State governments should change their roles within the education system, re-inventing themselves as facilitating and supervisory organisations. Teacher training, infrastructure and syllabuses need to be urgently upgraded. Industry should come forward to share experience with students and to offer more opportunities for live projects.

The free market philosophy has already entered the educational world in a big way. Commercialisation of education is the order of the day. Commercial institutions offering specialised education have come up everywhere. In view of globalisation, many corporate universities, both foreign and Indian, are encroaching upon our government institutions.

Our Institutes like IIMs and IITs have produced world class professionals. These institutes imparts quality education as per industry expectations and give due importance to Institute Industry Interface. Under the new scenario, Public-Private Partnership is becoming important in Management Education. Now India is a transforming country. We are near to achieve the status of developed nation.

Management Education is becoming increasingly important and the most sought after post-graduate degree among graduates. Any developing country for its economic and social development requires well-qualified managers and administrators. Also industry requires competent managers all the times, in times of secession and in times of growth. Management Education, therefore, is evergreen with job opportunities. However, to what extent our management graduates are getting the right type of Management Education. Indian Industry Survey reports that only 15 per cent of Management graduates are employable and 85 per cent unemployable. Management programmes offered by many universities and colleges suffer from serious drawbacks.

Some of the situations that have arisen in post liberalisation India are:

- Shifting of Agricultures to industry
- Urbanisation
- Opening up of trade market export import boom
- Big open saturated market for products
- Growing market for high quality and low price product
- Gradual increase of organised retail chain
- Growing number of Merger and Acquisition

- Lucid license policies for overseas Multinational corporations
- High growth is showing economic prosperity
- Indian market leaders going global

Challenges

1. The current curriculum in management education does not teach students in facing the challenges in business environment.
2. How to manage uncertainly and complexity are not taught in business schools.
3. It merely teaches the concepts with case studies.
4. It does not focus on the challenges arising out of rapid growing technology and the challenges involved in running on enterprise.
5. Unfortunately, the best talent is going to industry, where salaries are lucrative.
6. Those who come to academic area are the ones, who could not be absorbed in the industry or those who come to this profession by chance or those who chose this career out of passion.

Overcoming Challenges

- Re-engineering of management education must be done.
- Provide decent salaries and professional ambience to faculties.
- Send the faculty regularly for training programmes to update the skills and abilities.
- Develop right mindset and attitude. Focus on quality of education not quantity.
- There has to be interactive sessions for the student rather than mere preaching what is mentioned in the books.
- You cannot become a crack shot unless you lose some ammunition.
- The students have to be exposed to the industry through interface so that they understand the practical problem in corporate world. This boosts more confidence among the students.
- The project work should be contextual, relevant and should focus on the current scenarios.
- MBA is a professional degree and it should train and groom the students to be true professionals to take on the challenges being faced in the business environment.
- Make accreditation mandatory to ensure quality of education.
- Take stringent action against the illegal and unauthorised MBA colleges.
- Use online courses and other e-learning methods to increase training opportunities for field and local stuff.

- Provide training in languages besides English.
- Ensure that training is provided even in emergency situations.

New Skills require for future Global Managers

- Information Management Skill
- Information Technology Management Skill
- Decision-making in very dynamic environment
- H.R.D Skill
- Innovation/ Credibility
- Service Sector Management Skills
- Time Management Skills
- Stress Management Skills
- Environment Management Skills
- Entrepreneurship
- Customers Services Management Skills

Following the Global Standards

It is important that Management institutions in the country, adopt and follow the global standards of education and incorporate the following in their infrastructure and pedagogy as suggested by JKL University.

- Make management education student-centric, not faculty-centric
- Involve in Industry collaboration to tone up the practical skills of the students via internship/training.
- Organise regular practical training at a related management industry to help the students capture the right pulse.
- Craft the management curriculum in line with the latest industry trends, standards, and practices.
- Incorporate digital education, which is a must in the current scenario, whether to train students or the faculty.
- Have faculty with diversified experience. Gone are the days when the faculty used to remain restricted to just teaching. Today, they should diversify to training, research, and consultancy.
- Engaging students in seminars, etc., where industry experts impart them with current knowledge.
- *Globalise Education*: This can only be done by collaborating with foreign universities. India's upgraded education policy will go a long way to help to do this.
- Replace most of the theory-based education slowly yet steadily with practical-based education as only this comes handy when the students look for jobs in the corporate world outside.

- *R&D based collaboration:* Constant research and development, weather in the industry or its related education, is a must and thus it is important that the curriculum at a management school keeps updating with the changing demands of the industry. This can be achieved only when a management school collaborates with the big-wigs of the industry to walk hand-in-hand to create world-class management graduates/ postgraduates.
- Creating new and better courses and customising them as per the interest of the industry as well as the students is the need of the current management education system. And if the Indian management education has to stay world-class, it has not only to challenge it but also reinvent itself from time to time to meet the modern needs of the dynamic global business environment.

20
Research

Research has always been viewed as a critical activity for a management school as it helps improve teaching by enabling the faculty members to effectively develop curricula and course content, and increase the intellectual capital of the institution as well as its reputation. An institution's strength in research lays a solid foundation for teaching and consultancy. Without a sound research base, management schools risk losing their relevance, utility and legitimacy.

Dismal State of Research

Many people have lamented the dismal state of research in management schools in India. Notably in 2011, the then Environment Minister of India Jairam Ramesh, went to the extent of saying that the premier institutions of India such as the IITs and HMS were not world-class but excellent because of the quality of students, and not because of quality of faculty research. Earlier in that year, educator Nirmalya Kumar, who was then at London Business School, pointed out the gloomy state of management research in India. In his study, for the period between 1990 and 2009, he could find only108 unique articles being published in a widely accepted list of 40 journals that the Financial Times uses for ranking research at business schools in its annual global MBA rankings.

Emphasis on Research

A research culture needs a research community and a research agenda. Such a culture will be created only when it becomes an organisational priority and there is top commitment for building that. If the targets of B-Schools are predominantly monetary, a research culture will not emerge. It is proposed that the enhanced support for research can be brought about in three ways, viz.

1. Certain themes that need special study in the coming years should be funded, and scholars should be invited to undertake research in those areas.
2. Research granting procedure should be seriously reviewed to support individual project proposals, and
3. Encouraging institutions that have adequate support systems to start Ph.D. programme.

Only the top twenty-thirty schools produce a credible research and publications output. Relative lack of innovation in pedagogy creates managers who are more likely to routine decisions as risk averse followers of the beaten track, rather than risk-takers and leaders. The management institutions do not provide conducive environment that is supportive to research. Management institutes need to work in this direction. Research not only leads to updation of knowledge in concerned subject, but also leads to knowledge creation. Promoting a research culture in a management institutes requires change of mind setup on the side of management. Research is a central part and collective endeavor of the academic mission of business schools. It moulds the thinking of researchers and advances the degree of knowledge conveyed in the classroom. The research outcomes ultimately determine the educational content of business schools around the world. Any successful attempt to transform the educational process must, therefore, consider the types of research that is necessary to support such transformation and produce the required body of knowledge. Management education ought to develop a "body of knowledge of substantial intellectual content" to answer critical management questions as well as a set of "standards of professional conduct, which take precedence over the goal of personal gain".

2009 AACSB Report on the impact of research has drawn attention to the three levels of research required of any professional discipline, namely, (i) basic, (ii) applied and (iii) pedagogical research.

i. Basic research is intended to contribute to the "stock of knowledge of business and management theory" and will normally be the subject of peer-reviewed publications targeted to other academics.
ii. Applied research refers to the "scholarship of application", that is, how existing knowledge and theories can help resolve important business and management problems. This type of research is intended to reach the world of practice and is often disseminated through professional journals and trade books.
iii. Finally, pedagogical research focuses on producing teaching materials and instructional.

World class Business Schools view academic research as a backbone that support the pedagogical mission. There are three reasons for this stands. First, academic research can lay the foundations for concepts that eventually influence practice. Second, the skills development by academic researchers are invaluable in providing a rigorous foundation for practitioners. Third, on a more pragmatic note, Business Schools complete for faculty talent and the smartest graduates from the leading doctoral programmes in business and management aspire to be thought leaders, not teachers. If a school does not support academic research, then attracting the best faculty is impossible.

IAM Conference

In 2011 summer, a group of five management scholars from both India and overseas felt that it would be a worthwhile idea to take stock of Indian management research and explore future directions by showcasing a symposium at the Second Indian Academy of Management Conference hosted by IIM-Bengaluru in December 2011. They included: Dr Pawan Budhwar, Aston Business School, UK; Dr Naresh Khatri, University of Missouri, USA; Dr Abhoy Ojha, IIM-Bengaluru; Dr Vasanthi Srinivasan, IIM-Bengaluru; and Dr Arup Varma, Loyola University USA.

The main issues of the symposium reflected several of the concerns that have been raised earlier. The initial list of questions that set the pace for developing the symposium proposal included the following: (i) Should scholars interested in India take US/Western theories as the basis and generalise them to India or should they develop new indigenous theories? (ii) Should Indian management research use the US/Western model in terms of journals, conferences, and measuring and rewarding research productivity? (iii) Would Indian management research be better served by emphasising publications in the so-called top-tier journals in the US/West or would it be better served by developing and improving management journals in India? (iv) How can a critical mass of management scholars and scholarship on India be created?

Current Condition of Research

There are several reasons for the current condition of research on management in India. Till very recently, research in almost any field in India was not valued by any of the domestic stakeholders, including governments, students and managers. Hence, most faculty members or practitioners were happy to rely on research done elsewhere. The dominant ethos of 'Universal' knowledge, which is very appropriate for the natural sciences was applied to the social sciences and the relevance of research from the West to the Indian context was rarely questioned. As a result, very few faculty members in management schools in India devoted significant energies towards original research and were happy to borrow knowledge developed outside the Indian context. The limited research efforts that were undertaken were further hampered by inadequate training, lacks of interesting in conducting research and also a lack of incentives in the Indian system to support and/or reward research. But most important, was the lack of confidence in the Indian researcher to assert his/her stand if did not conform to the received wisdom from the developed world.

Indian Academy of Management (IAM) Services

The Indian Academy of Management (IAM) has been created to provide a global platform for management scholars in India and elsewhere to network collaborate, and conduct research on India. The booming economy and increasingly important geopolitical position of India, coupled with limited good quality research on India as attracting attention from scholars all over the globe. As a result, lately, there has been a big surge in journal publications and books on India. Editors of leading journals and publishing houses, who were historically much less receptive to India, have begun showing keen interest in publishing research on India. Realising the need to support, acknowledge, and facilitate the creation and dissemination of Indian management research, Academy of Management, USA, in 2011 accepted IAM as one of its affiliates. IAM can (i) spearhead the creation and dissemination of overseas; (ii) influence business and management policy and education; and (iii) act as a resource to develop the next generation of researchers.

As IAM continues to evolve, it should be able to provide a range of useful and much needed avenues and services to its members. Examples of these can be: (i) building a strong and active community of scholars on India, who can meet on a regular basis to share their findings, research ideas, proposals, and discuss challenges and how to meet them ii) establishing a journal on Indian management research for the creation and dissemination of knowledge on Indian businesses and organisations; (iii) linking with other professional bodies based not only in India but also globally such as the Academy of International Business; (iv) delivering developmental programmes for early career researchers (such as how to publish in leading journals or write research grants)and professional development programmes targeted at senior academics working inkey research positions such as directors of research; (v) creating an active interface between academic scholars and practitioners via different network events and conferences; (vi) assisting academic institutions in developing their research ethics policies; (vii) being a repository of e-based literature; and (viii) acting as an interface between different India related research centers spread across countries.

Unique Style of Research

Indian business education and schools need to face the reality that the quantity of teaching and classroom instruction depends largely on the body of knowledge on which it is based. The solutions to a number of management problems that Indian organisations face are likely to be quite different from North American organisations because of India's unique history, culture and social system, as well as India being in a different phase of development. Thus, Indian management research and teaching should lead to presenting to the world a style of management, which uniquely expresses the Indian socio-cultural heritage, combined with the current frontiers in management.

Indian management scholarship has to develop greater self-confidence. While it needs to have a healthy respect for Western scholarship, it would be counterproductive to follow it blindly. North American management research has its own problems. Currently a debate in North American research community is raging about its relevance to management practice.

Indian management scholarship needs to develop a unique research culture. Learning from North American research is undoubtedly valuable but imitating it is not. We are not sure if the model that some of the universities in Asia, such as Hong Kong University of Science and Technology, National Taiwan University, National University of Singapore, and Indian School of Business, are following will serve Indian management education and practice well.

Several reasons have been attributed for the non-performance of business school faculty on research which range from lack of faculty competence, weak eco system to promote research, lack of good infrastructure to do research, funding constraints and finally, the lack of incentives for faculty to do research. While all these arguments have some merit, the key question that one needs to ask is, 'How does one build a research culture in an organisation where the DNA has historically been shaped by teaching?' At this stage, it must be understood that the role of teaching is not being undermined in any manner. While teaching has been in the foreground and research in the background in business schools for several decades now, the time has come for research to take centre stage and feature in the foreground in the immediate future. How do business schools in India manage this transition to a research culture? In particular, how can the Human Resource (HR) systems and processes in a business school enable this transition in an effective manner?

Producing World Class Research

Management scholars should ensure that they produce only world-class research. One good way to ensure this is to submit manuscripts to international journals. The reviews at leading journals are often extremely detailed and helpful, and can help guide authors in modifying their manuscripts to global standards. This should be relatively easy for senior scholars who do not have the pressures that junior scholars often face (publish or perish). In addition, senior scholars should mentor junior scholars and also convince administrators and the powers-that-be to insist on quality research, rather than quantity. Clearly, research that has no impact is not necessary and serves little purpose. In addition, junior scholars should seek out partnerships with senior scholars around the world to collaborate on and co-author research. This will help them publish in quality journals, as well as learn the ropes of publishing in international journals.

Research in Faculty Quality

There is no evidence of research in the area of faculty quality in B-Schools in India. Reasons for poor performance of B-Schools need to be studied further like investment in training and development of faculty, faculty interactions with industry and preparedness of industry to invest financial resources to aid research in the area of management and finding innovative solutions through research. An insight into the talent management practices like attracting, identifying and retaining talent is necessary to understand the reasons for disconnect between skills shortage and unemployment. Faculty quality is best understood through the efficient implementation of performance management systems like goal setting process, performance appraisals and metrics used for measurement of performance. Metrics could include success of students in placement interviews, learning of students to make effective transition into leaders and managers capable of delivery value to corporate organisations. More research data is required to study effectiveness of training of faculty and their ability to deliver value to students. Measurement of performance and reward management systems of B-Schools to attract quality faculty and the efforts of the B-Schools in this regard has to be evaluated through data driven research.

Case Research is Vital

Management schools should focus on qualitative research and research in pedagogy. Management education is quite different from other disciplines. Case research is vital for management both for theory development as well as for preparation of teaching cases for classroom use. In a 2018 article, *Harvard Business*, School Professors Nitin Nohria and Jan W. Rivkin wrote "Comparative case based research has yielded some of the most influential ideas in business scholarship. Writing cases brings scholars closer to management practice, which increasingly has become a priority among business schools." Development of teaching cases along with comprehensive teaching notes should be given due weightage as these go a long way in contributing to keeping the curricula and course content relevant. A premier accreditation body such as Association to Advance Collegiate Schools of Business(AACSB) has recognised the importance of teaching cases and is looking at ways to recognise management schools for their case research efforts. It is high time that case research got its due recognition in disciplines like management, where the application of knowledge is critical to evaluating its impact. Management schools in India, accreditation, ranking and rating bodies in India should also look at ways in which to recognise this form of research.

21
Overseeing Organisations

AICTE

There are many reasons for the wide difference in quality of business education in India, one important reason is likely to be the absence of a body that all institutions look up to set standards— like the AACSB in USA. Although there is an apex body – the All India Council of Technical Education (AICTE) that is responsible for defining the basic framework for quality of the business education and approving entry and expansion of all institutions, there are in practice, many problems that undermine its effectiveness.

In order to install the quality in the management education in India, the AICTE, apex institution in the country and universities should focus on the following issues:

- Quality Assurance
- Qualifies and Competent faculty
- Proper Infrastructure
- Accountability of Management Institutes
- Faculty Shortages
- Values and Ethics
- Allowing Foreign Institutes in India
- Role of Professional Bodies and Authorities etc.

Task cut out for AICTE

In the years to come, the demand and supply conditions concerned with MBA is going to see a mismatch. The AICTE should act tough on certain key issue like:

a) It cannot allow any number of new entrants. Perhaps a restriction such as to allow only hundred new management schools of quality to come up in the next six years.
b) It should permit some good mid-level Business Schools to increase their intake capacity from the existing ones.
c) It should also consider encouraging some of the leading corporate to establish their own management schools.
d) AICTE should make each and every college accountable for all the information that they provide in the prospectus.
e) Should AICTE go for "A", "B" and "C" categorisation in accreditation of Business Schools or opt for a simpler system of say, "accredited", "not accredited" and "not applied for"?

f) What should be the role of government? Professional Association bodies like AIMS, AIU?
g) What should be the objective of Accreditation – "is it quality improvement" or "public awareness"?

Does the need of the hour is to make AICTE an Institutions created by an Act of Parliament?

This call for recognising the AICTE's Management Education as a profession established and approved independently by a special act of Parliament, with the objectives of promoting, regulating, and developing the profession of Management education. Just like The Institute of Cost and Works Accountants of India as the only recognised statutory professional organisation and licensing body in India specialising exclusively in Cost and Management Accountancy, AICTE must be made and start functioning in line with one such an Institution.

Objectives of one such an AICTE Act could be

a) To develop the Management Education function as a powerful tool of management control in all spheres of economic activities.
b) To promote and develop the adoption of scientific methods in modern management education.
c) To develop the professionals' body of members (viz., all MBA's passing-out of any of the AICTE recognised B-Schools) and equip them fully to discharge their functions and fulfill the objectives of the Institute in the context of the developing economy.
d) To keep abreast of the latest developments in the management education principles and practices, to incorporate such changes are essential for sustained vitality of the industry and other economic activities.
e) To exercise supervision for the entrants to the profession and to ensure strict adherence to the best ethical standards by the profession.
f) To organise seminars and conferences on subjects of professional interest in different parts of the country for cross-fertilisation of ideas for professional growth.
g) To carry out research and publication activities covering various economic spheres and the publishing of books and booklets for spreading information of professional interest to members in industrial, education and commercial units in India and abroad.

Need for adequacy of qualified input resources

Following crucial aspects, which make a quality management institute form the Input Resource.

Faculty: The institute must have permanent or regular faculty in all the main areas of Management like Marketing, Human Resources, Economics, Information Technology, Accounting and Finance, Quantitative Methods and Production.

Each of these faculty members must meet at least one of the three criteria - senior managerial experience with a leading organisation along with ability to relate the same to the management concepts, consultancy experience in the corporate world and research experience in management. If the faculties were simply graduates, post-graduates or Ph.D. without meeting this criterion then they would be just teaching the theories from the books which are not really relevant for a managerial career. Management career is about practice of management, which can be taught only by experience, expertise and exposure together-with the relevant concepts.

Facilities: The infrastructure and facilities must include classrooms with multimedia and projection facilities, latest computers and peripherals and a good library with collection of books on all management subjects.

Courses and Programmes: The courses and programmes must be in line with the requirements of the corporate world and other organisations. It means these must have regular inputs incorporated from these organisations and not based on some books authored by someone who never had any exposure to the management career, consultancy or research.

Networking: The institute must have extensive networking with the corporate world and other organisations nationally and internationally.

This networking, on the one hand, makes it possible for the regular interaction of their senior managerial personnel with the students while on the other hand, provides these organisations a platform to assess the institute being equipped to develop the required capability in the students.

This also enables these organisations to consider the students for placement when they complete the programme.

Few of the Issues to be addressed as FAQ's...

Q's: Have the B-Schools been adapting quickly enough to the changing demands of the students and their future employers?

Facts: The biggest change over the last 20 years lies in the professional interests of our students. If the median dream of a Michigan MBA student 20 or 25 years ago was to be CEO of Ford Motor Co., today the dream is to start a business, have an ownership stake, or create economic value for themselves and others. In school, they want to understand how to write business plans, how to get financing, and how to manage a growing enterprise. They don't just want to hear about it from the faculty, they want hands-on experience.

Q's: There are some people out there in the society for whom a top business education would be an enormous help, and we're not serving them well enough. Women is one group. On average, there are a few exceptions, at top business schools, 25 per cent-30 per cent of the class is made up of women. Meanwhile, women who are streaming into law school, streaming into medical school, and majority of them streaming into profession, but not even 10 per cent of MBA's turn to entrepreneurship?

Facts: Business schools haven't reached out and made themselves very attractive to women as a career path compared with other professions, such as law and medicine. I don't think we're getting the word out to women that business is a path to economic independence. We've done a poor job in marketing to them.* Also there is very lesser participation in our programme, by economically backward but talented students. What's the next challenge? It's an economic empowerment issue. Top MBA programme is a gateway to economic opportunity and to privilege and responsibility. I am sure that none of us is satisfied with the representation of economically backward students and rural background students in our programme. We are under-serving important parts of our society, people who would really benefit from a top MBA education. And looking over the next few years, we ought to work individually and together to bring this opportunity to more people who would benefit from it.

National Board of Accreditation (NBA)

There are two central bodies involved in accreditation: the National Accreditation and Assessment Council (NAAC) and the National Board of Accreditation (NBA). The NAAC was set up in by the University Grants Commission for institutional accreditation through a combination of internal and external quality assessment.

The NBA was originally constituted in September 1994 to assess the qualitative competence of the educational institutions from diploma level to postgraduate level in engineering and technology, management, pharmacy, architecture, and related disciplines. The NBA, in its present form, has come into existence as an autonomous body with effect from 7th January 2010, with the objective of assurance of quality and relevance of the technical education through the mechanisms of accreditation of programmes offered by the technical institutions.

The NBA works very closely with stakeholders (faculty, educational institutions, government, industries, regulators, management, students, recruiters, alumni and their parents) to ensure that the programmes serve to prepare their graduates with sound knowledge of fundamentals and to develop in them an adequate level of professional competence, such as would meet the needs of the engineering profession locally as well as globally. The objective of the NBA is to assess and accredit institutions as well as professional programmes offered at various levels by the technical institutions on the basis of norms prescribed by the NBA.

The vision of the NBA is "to be an accrediting agency of international repute by ensuring the highest degree of credibility in assurance of quality and relevance of professional education and *fulfill* the expectations of its stakeholders, viz., *academicians;* corporate, educational institutions, government, industry, regulators, students, and *their* parents.

The NBA is working with the mission, to stimulate the quality of teaching, self-evaluation, and accountability in the higher education system, which help institutions realise their academic objectives and adopt teaching practices that enable them to produce high-quality professionals and to assess and accredit the programmes offered by the colleges or the institutions, or both, imparting technical and professional education.

Main Objectives of the NBA are to

a) assess and grade colleges and/or institutions of technical and professional education, the courses and programmes offered by them, their various units, faculty, departments etc.,
b) stimulate the academic environment and quality of teaching and research in these institutions,
c) contribute to the sphere of knowledge in its discipline ,
d) motivate colleges and/or institutions of technical and professional education for research, and adopt teaching practices that groom their students for the innovation and development of leadership qualities,
e) encourage innovation, self-evaluation and accountability in higher education,
f) promote necessary changes, innovation and reforms in all aspects of the working of the colleges/institutions of technical and professional education for the above purpose, and
g) help institutions to realise their academic objectives.

Authorities of the NBA

At present, the NBA has the following authorities.

I. The General Council
II. The Executive Committee
III. The President

Accreditation

Accreditation is a process of quality assurance and improvement, whereby an Institute/ or a programme offered by an Institution is critically appraised to verify that the institution or the programme continues to meet and exceed the norms and standards prescribed by the appropriate designated authorities. Accreditation does not seek to replace the system of award of degree and diplomas by the universities] Institutions. But, accreditation provides quality assurance that the academic aims and objectives of the Institution are honestly pursued, and effectively achieved by the resources available, and that the institution has demonstrated capabilities of ensuring effectiveness of the educational programmes over the validity period of accreditation. NBA accreditation is a quality assurance scheme for higher technical education.

Significance of Accreditation

- To make the institute/department aware of the weaknesses of the programme offered by it and act on suggestions for improvement.
- To encourage the institute to move continuously towards the improvement of quality of its programme, and the pursuit of excellence.
- To facilitate institutions for updating themselves in programme curriculum, teaching and learning processes, faculty achievements, and student's skills/abilities/knowledge.
- To excel among stakeholders (peers, students, employers, societies etc.).
- To facilitate receiving of grants from Government regulatory bodies and institutions/agencies.
- To attain international recognition of accredited degrees awarded.
- To facilitate the mobility of graduated students and professionals.

Accreditation Policy

The following general policies are the guiding principles for the accreditation of Business Schools:

i. Educational institutions are accredited at present.
ii. Business schools to be accredited should be those which have been formally approved by the appropriate designated authority or authorities, as the case may be.
iii. Business schools which have produced postgraduates for at least two academic years will be considered for full accreditation and, provisional accreditation, as the case may be.
iv. Business schools will be considered for assessment and accreditation only at the written request of the educational institution and after agreeing to abide by the NBA_s accreditation manual, rules, regulations and notification issued from time to time.
v. Accreditation will normally be granted for a specific term of up to a maximum of five academic years. Provisional accreditation may also be granted to new business schools (not matured for full accreditation).

vi. After accreditation, the institutions are expected to submit their annual self-assessment report to eNBA online. If any aspect of the programme is found to be sufficiently unsatisfactory and/or does not comply with norms, the NBA reserves the right to revoke the accreditation. If necessary, the NBA may appoint a maximum of two members to form an Evaluation Team to act as mentors at the request of institution. The mentor(s) may visit the educational institution at its request for mentoring purposes and provide a report to the NBA on their findings for each visit. The educational institution will bear the expenses of the visit and pay honorarium to the mentors as prescribed by the NBA.

vii. Accreditation is based on satisfying the minimum standards.

viii. All correspondence between the educational institution and the NBA vis-a-vis accreditation process is confidential and may not be revealed to any unauthorised persons under any circumstances, except with written permission from the concerned educational institution.

ix. A three day onsite visit shall be a part of the accreditation process. An evaluation team appointed by the NBA will carry out the evaluation of the business school. The evaluation team consists of evaluators and is headed by a chairperson. The institute shall propose such set of dates for visit when the regular classes and all academic activities are on.

x. The final decision made by the NBA will be communicated to the educational institution together with comments which portray strengths, weaknesses and scope for improvement. In the event that a business school is not accredited, reasons for the decision will also be given. If accreditation is denied and if the educational institution wishes, it may appeal against the decision to the Appellate Committee (AC).

xi. The educational institution shall bear the cost of accreditation, as per the fee prescribed by the NBA.

Association of Indian Management Schools (AIMS)

The Association of Indian Management Schools (AIMS) is a networking body of B-Schools in India for professional development of management education and safeguarding the interests of B-Schools in the country.

30 years ago, in the context of the policy implications arising from the National Education Policy of 1986 (which advocated expansion of "Open University System" and recognised "rural university" model), a National Conference of Heads of Management Institutions was held at Bengaluru from 28th to 30th April, 1988 where it was resolved that "a Network of Management Institutions offering Post-Graduate Courses be constituted". Pursuant to this resolution, the Association of Indian Management Schools

(AIMS), a non-profit-making society was registered on 27th August, 1988 under the Karnataka Societies Registration Act of 1960.

As an independent networking body, AIMS can now boast of having many top class institutions like IIMs, ISB, ASCI, Xavier Institutions, Welingkar Institute of Management (WeSchool), NMIMS, ICFAI, MDI, S P Jain and many management departments of Universities as its members. It is the official representative of Indian Management Schools in India as well as in some important international forums. It is one of the largest networking bodies of B-Schools in the world.

Vision

To function as the true representative body of Management Education in India, for safeguarding the interests of the sector and contributing to quality improvement on a continuing basis.

To make determined efforts to develop and project its identity as the national network of Management Schools in India.

Mission

Its mission is to function as a professional association of management education concerned with:

- Quality of management education in India
- Faculty training and development
- Management research
- Curriculum development
- Help maintain and improve standards of teaching, research and examination.
- Help in the accreditation process of Management Education institutions
- And take all such steps on its own or in collaboration with other agencies for the promotion of Management Education in India.

Structure of AIMS

AIMS has a General Body comprising all the Institutional Members and an Executive Board consisting of the President, Vice-President, Treasurer, Immediate Past President and nine other members, elected by the General Body of Institutional Members.

All the former Presidents attend the meetings of the Executive Board as invitees without voting rights.

Creation of Regional Councils and Chapters

During 2009, in view of persistent demand from AIMS members to strengthen the set-up and also bring in the element of democratisation through the process of elections and widening of the base at local and regional level, the following structure was adopted:

> "There would be a three-tier, federal decentralised structure of governance with strong central collective leadership and coordination system. This may consist of National and Regional bodies and Local chapters."

General Body > Executive Board > Regional Councils > Local Chapters

Pursuant to the above decision, a total of 15 Chapters have been formed and based on elections/nominations, the office bearers of the Chapter Managing Committees will be filled.

AIMS Activities

Policy Advocacy: One of the core objectives of AIMS is its policy advocacy role in safeguarding the interests of business schools in India. Therefore, it is officially represented in different bodies of Government of India connected with Management Education. In line with its policy, AIMS fought a case against AICTE regulations issued in December 2010 to be observed by management institutes in regard to admission process, tests, fees, etc and has been successful in getting most of the issues decreed by the Supreme Court in favour of the institutes. It keeps on representing to the Government of India and others for solving regulatory issues being faced by management institutions.

Programmes by AIMS in association with Member Institutions

AIMS conduct a number of Faculty Development Programmes, Industry Institution Interface and National and International Conferences, Programmes on Leading India in Management Education, Round Tables of Deans and Directors of Management Institutions in the country.

It lends financial support to its member institutions for conducting various national and international seminars, conferences or workshops or faculty development programmes, case writing and research programmes.

Many national and international seminars/conferences are sponsored by AIMS on highly critical themes like: Quality of Management Education, Accreditation, Ranking of Business Schools, Industry-B-Schools Interface, Leading India in Management Education (LIME), Research Methodology, Case Writing and Presentations and so on.

Further, there are round tables of Deans and Directors focusing on various subjects of topical interest to them. Extensive financial support is extended to them also. Thus, AIMS helps in active participation of its member institutions – their deans/directors, faculty and students.

AIMS Annual Convention

AIMS flagship event is its Annual Management Education Convention on a topic of current interest to management institutions, management faculty/

students, industry and government. It is normally held at the place from where the President is elected and organised by the Institution that s/he belongs.

AIMS Convention is a platform where well-known political leaders, national and international academicians, heads of management education institutions, faculty and students exchange their valuable views, opinions and experiences for the benefit of the audience.

Awards given at the Convention

- AIMS-RCM Best B-School Director Award
- AIMS J L Batra Best Research Paper Award
- AIMS Best Case Award
- AIMS Best Student Paper Award
- AIMS-WeSchool Innovation Award
- AIMS-ICFAI Best Teacher Award
- AIMS Ramaswamy P Aiyar Best Young Teacher Award
- AIMS National Management Week Award
- Ravi J Matthai National Fellow Award: This is a prestigious award which is presented during the AIMS Annual Convention to management educators and professionals for achieving a high level of distinction in their respective discipline
- Research Papers: AIMS invites unpublished, empirical, high quality research papers from practicing Managers, Academicians, Research Scholars and Entrepreneurs for presentation at the Convention and publication in the Souvenir.

AIMS Journal of Management, UGC approved, is a half-yearly journal which contains articles on the issues of current interest in management. It publishes empirical or conceptual papers, research notes, case studies and book-reviews. It is distributed to all its members and some important libraries in India and abroad. The editorial board comprises of eminent academics well-versed in the art of screening and selecting articles for journals.

AIMS brings out a bi-monthly eNews letter covering important news and events of AIMS and member institutions and circulates it to all members.

Networking with Global B-School Networks

AIMS has a few tie-ups with international bodies like Association of Management Development Institutions in South Asia (AMDISA), Accreditation Council for Business Schools and Programmes (ACBSP), European Foundation for Management Development (EFMD). The President and a few Members attend their annual conferences and participate in their deliberations.

Such interactions at a global level are a must for improving quality management education in India. AIMS has been inviting international academic experts to its convention, seminars and conferences to facilitate stakeholders of management education gain insights into global management education.

22

UGC New Regulations

For Recognition and Monitoring of Assessment and Agencies

At present, there is only one agency for the assessment and accreditation of all Higher Educational Institutions (HEL) in the country viz., National Assessment and Accreditation Council (NAAC) established in 1994. National Board for Accreditation (NBA) is also taking up similar exercise but it is confined to the HHS offering engineering/technology programmes of studies — focusing more on the Department-wise assessment and accreditation. NAAC is also undertaking the assessment and accreditation of engineering/technology colleges (institutional assessment and accreditation).Consequently, for all practical purposes, there is only one agency for the entire country for the assessment and accreditation of HEIs.

It may be noted here that the number of HEIs has been increasing continuously and substantially. These HEIs include about 907 universities (central universities: 48; state universities: 399; deemed-to-be universities: 126; and private universities: 334) and about 39,050 colleges. Out of these HELs, only about 7,800 institutions are assessed and accredited. Though NAAC has been striving hard, it has not been able to complete the assessment and accreditation of all HEIs. Limited capacity of NAAC, inadequate number of assessors (experts) and HEIs not taking interest to get them assessed and accredited, etc., are some of the reasons. Further, there is no end for the work of accreditation agencies as it is continuous, after first assessment and accreditation, the institutions go in for reassessment/reaccreditation, usually, after every five years.

In the light of large number of HEIs to be assessed and accredited/ reaccredited, the University Grants Commission (UGC/Commission) has realised the need for expanding/ enhancing the existing capacity of assessment and accreditation agency (ies). Hence, the UGC has decided to recognise more entities/agencies to assess and accredit HEIs in the country. In this backdrop, the Commission has finalised and notified the Regulations called, University Grants Commission (Recognition and Monitoring of Assessment and Accreditation Agencies) Regulations, 2018. These Regulations are in suppression of the earlier ones.

Though most of the terms are familiar to the stakeholders of HEIs, certain terms are new and they are used frequently in these Regulations. Therefore, the meanings of a few new terms, as provided in the Regulations, are:

Assessment and Accreditation Agency (AAA) is an agency registered under these Regulations for the purpose of taking up the assessment and accreditation of HEIs. These AAAs include even the NAAC and NBA. Accreditation Advisory Council (AAC) is the Council to be constituted by the UGC for the purpose of rendering advisory services to the Commission on important aspects such as recommendation of AAA to the Commission for registration, fees to be levied on the HEIs for assessment and accreditation, etc. Government Agency means an entity/institution owned and funded by the Central and/or State Government/s. Semi Government Agency represents an entity/institution formed by a government agency (with majority stake) in a partnership with a private entity which has at least five years of experience in the accreditation process. Certificate of Registration (CoR) means the certificate of registration of an AAA granted by the Commission on the recommendation of AAC.

The primary objective of these Regulations is to lay down a framework for mandatory assessment and accreditation of HEIs (including technical education programmes) and allowing setting up of AAAs by the government or semi-government agencies (apart from the existing accreditation institutions viz., NAAC and NBA). These Regulations specify not only the procedure and criteria for registration of AAAs but also aim at regulating them (i.e., AAAs) through independent but accountable institutional mechanism-by laying down a code of ethics, undertaking audit of work and accounts of AAAs, specifying the fees livable for carrying out assessment and accreditation, etc. The Commission (in consultation with the AAC) lays down the norms and procedures for assessment and accreditation of HEIs (or programmes including technical education programmes) by the AAAs.

These Regulations are applicable to all AAAs engaged in the assessment and accreditation of HEIs in the county and/or programmes of studies offered by them.

Accreditation Advisory Council (AAC)

In order to advise the Commission about various aspects pertaining to AAAs, and assessment and accreditation of HEIs, these Regulations empower the Commission to set up an Accreditation Advisory Council (AAC) with not more than 10 members. The persons to be nominated to the Council as the members shall be distinguished academicians, and/or experts in the area of higher education, and assessment and accreditation. By following a transparent and merit-based evaluation procedure, the Council is required to recommend the entities/agencies to the Commission for registration as AAAs. And based on the recommendation of AAC, the Commission notifies the 52-AAAs. Besides, AAC advises/helps the Commission in developing and regulating the process of assessment and accreditation of HEIs and the programmes offered by them, and in monitoring the functioning/working of AAAs.

Registration of AAAs

For the purpose of identifying the agencies/entities capable of taking up the assessment and accreditation of I-IEIs, the Commission issues a public notification inviting eligible and willing government and semi-government entities to submit their applications with necessary documents and fees.

The applicant (i.e. the agency submitting application for recognition by the Commission as an approved/registered AAA) shall be a government or semi- government agency and registered as a company or as a society formed and registered under the Societies Registration Act, or trust formed under the Indian trust Act or any other law for the time being in force.

Applications received by the Commission (in response to its notification) will be sent to AAC for assessment and advice. And the AAC is required to complete the evaluation process about the suitability and competency of each of the applicants within 30 days (from the date of receipt of applications). Based on the scrutiny and evaluation of applications, it (i.e., AAC) shall submit its report to the Commission recommending specifically whether the applicants can be granted the Certificate of Registration (CoR) or it/they can be rejected. Within 30 days from the receipt of recommendation from the AAC, the Commission shall issue the CoR of an AAA on such terms and conditions or reject the application for reasons to be recorded in writing. While issuing the CoR, the Commission shall also approve the procedure and conditions for assessment and accreditation specified by the AAA with or without modifications. Of course, the existing agencies in the field of assessment and accreditation viz., NAAC and NBA stand recognised (for the purposes of these Regulations). These Regulations specify that only those AAAs which are recognised by the Commission (for the purposes of these Regulations) are eligible to take up the assessment and accreditation of HEIs.

Further, the Regulations require the Commission and its AAC to develop comprehensive procedure and processes to be followed by the AAAs in the assessment and accreditation of HEIs or any programme conducted therein.

Initially, a CoR IS granted for a period of two years. And the subsequent (recognition) renewal is for a period of (every) three years.

Duties/ Obligations of AAA

While undertaking the assessment and accreditation of HEIs (or programmes conducted therein), the AAA is required to observe certain principles. These principles include, among others, (i) advancement of academic quality,

(ii) enabling uniform reference of standards of academic quality in any classes of HEIs or any programmes including technical education programmes conducted therein, (iii) informing stakeholders about the quality of HEIs academic/research programmes conducted therein, (iv) rendering assistance/service to HEIs in managing and enhancing their academic quality and work toward the development of explicit intended learning outcomes, etc.

Further, the AAA is required to base the assessment and accreditation of HEIs on verifiable data (on performance yardsticks) which are to be publicly disclosed. It should also consider the views of stakeholders of HEIs such as students and employees, and also the objections/suggestions of HEIs while finalising the assessment and accreditation of such institution (s) or programmes conducted therein. These measures are necessary to ensure transparency in the process of assessment and accreditation of HEIs.

AAAs are also required to submit the necessary reports about the institutions assessed and accredited by them, and the statements of accounts on yearly basis to the Commission. The accounts of all AAAs are subject to audit by the office of the Comptroller and Auditor General (CAG) of India.

While submitting application for assessment and accreditation, HEIs have an option to indicate three choices of AAAs. Based on preferences, the AAC takes the decision about the allocation of an AAA for a HEI considering all relevant factors. And the decision of AAC is final and binding on both the HEI and the AAA concerned.

Any party/person aggrieved by the assessment/accreditation decided by any AAA under these Regulations may submit its grievance to the Commission for withdrawal of such assessment/accreditation, or for its modification. The Commission shall take a final decision on the grievance received within 90 days after providing a reasonable opportunity to the AAA of being heard and after due consultation with the AAC.

If any AAA resorts to corrupt/unlawful practices or if it is found to have given accreditation without due process, or if it has given rating based on extraneous considerations, such AAA can be debarred from further accreditation work by the AAC, apart from withdrawal of registration.

If an AAA fails to comply with the obligations and to adhere to the code of ethics, it shall be liable to pay such compensation to the HEI for any loss or damages suffered by such institution, as may be determined by a Court of Law. The Commission shall publish the name and address of the erring AAA in the Public Domain.

Any AAA which contravenes (i) any Provision of these Regulations; or (ii) the standards specified under any law by the appropriate statutory/regulatory authority; or (iii) the terms and conditions specified in the CoR shall be liable to a penalty as per the Provisions of the UGC Act, 1956.

Similarly, if any person provides any information or produces any document or delivers an account or statement which is false, he shall be liable for being prosecuted in a court of law by the Commission.

If any HEI furnishes false/misleading information or tries to influence the AAA in whatever way to obtain a high grade it shall be liable to be de-notified by UGC Act, 1956 and stoppage of/or withdrawal of UGC grants, if any. Similarly, a deemed-to-be-university shall be liable for de-notification of its status as a deemed-to-be-university under Section 3 of the UGC Act, 1956.

It is obvious from the above that there is a need for expanding the capacity of assessment and accreditation agencies. As the scope for expanding the capacity of existing agency/ies is limited, it is necessary to identify and recognise new entities/agencies to take up the assessment and accreditation work.

Positive Impact of New Regulations

- Faster rate of Accreditation
- Shared Accreditation load
- More innovation into Accreditation space
- Competition among Accreditation Agencies
- Wider Accreditation chances for HEIs

Appendix - 1
Top Accreditation Councils in India

1. UGC (University Grants Commission)

University Grants Commission (India) is statuary body set up by the Indian Union government in accordance with the UGC Act 1956 under Ministry of Human Resource Development and is charged with coordination, determination, and maintenance of standards of higher education. It provides recognition to universities in India and disburses funds to such recognised universities and colleges. It also advises the Central and State Governments on the measures which are necessary for the development of Higher Education. UGC was modeled after University Grants Committee of UK that was an advisory committee of the British government and advised on the distribution of grant funding amongst the British universities. Currently, *UGC conducts NET (National Eligibility Test)* for appointments of teachers in colleges and universities along with CSIR. Since 2009 NET qualification is mandatory for teaching at Graduation and Post-Graduation level.

2. AICTE (All India Council for Technical Education)

All India Council for Technical Education is the statutory body and a national-level council for technical education under Department of Higher Education, Ministry of Human Resource development that was first established in November 1945 as an advisory body. AICTE is responsible for proper planning and coordinated development of the technical education and management education system in India and also accredits postgraduate and graduate programmes under specific categories. It grants approval for starting new technical institutions, the introduction of new courses and variation in intake capacity in technical institutions. Every year as per the direction of Ministry of Human Resource development (MHRD), Government of India AICTE conducts a national level entrance examination called CMAT (Common Management Admission Test). A score of CMAT is accepted by all AICTE-Approved institutions/University Department/Constituent Colleges/Affiliated Colleges.

3. AIU (Association of Indian Universities)

Association of Indian Universities was formed in 1925 with an idea of bringing together all the universities on a common platform emerged from the deliberations of a Conference of the Vice Chancellors of Universities convened by Lord Reading, the then Viceroy of India at Shimla. It is an organisation and association of major universities that is based in Delhi that evaluates the courses, syllabi, standards and credits of foreign Universities pursued abroad and equates them in relation to various courses offered by Indian Universities. The AIU is mainly concerned with the recognition of Degrees/ Diplomas awarded by the Universities in India, which are recognised by the University Grants Commission, New Delhi, and abroad for the purpose of admission to higher degree courses in Indian Universities. IT is also a registered society under the Societies Registration Act, 1860 with the membership of Indian Universities. It acts as a bureau of information exchange in higher education and brings out a number of useful publications, including the Universities Handbook, research papers and a weekly journal titled University News. It is also empowered to grant Associate Membership to universities of the neighboring countries of India.

4. ICAI(Institute of Chartered Accountants of India)

The Institute of Chartered Accounts of India is the national professional accounting body of India established on July 1, 1949. It was formed under the Chartered Accounts Act, 1949 to regulate the profession of Chartered accountancy in India. ICAI is the only licensing cum regulating body in India of financial audit and accountancy profession. It is also the second largest professional Accounting and Finance body in the world in terms of membership, after American Institute of Certified Public Accountants. Any member wanting to engage in public practice has to first apply for and obtain a Certificate of Practice from the Council of ICAI as only these candidates can act as auditors or certify documents required by various tax and financial regulatory authorities in India.

5. ICSI (Institute of Company Secretaries of India)

The Institute of Company Secretaries of India is only recognised professional body in India to develop and regulate the profession of Company Secretaries that was constituted under the Company Secretaries Act, 1980. It awards the certificate of bestowing the designation of Company Secretary(CS) to a candidate qualifying for the membership of the Institute. The ICSI functions under the jurisdiction of Ministry of Corporate Affairs. It registers students with 10+2 and graduate qualifications for Foundation and Executive Programme of Company Secretaryship, respectively with course contents in Corporate and Economic Laws, Management, Accounting, Taxation and Finance disciplines.

6. FTII (Film and Television Institute of India)

The Film and Television Institute of India is an autonomous institute under the Ministry of Information and Broadcasting of the Government of India that is aided by the Central Government of India. It is also a member of the leading schools of film and television in the world known as the International Liaison Centre of Schools of Cinema and Television (CILECT). The FTII is registered under Societies' Registration Act of 1860. IT also conducts FTII Entrance Examination for the candidates who wish to pursue their career in Film and television industry.

7. NAAC (National Assessment and Accreditation Council)

National Assessment and Accreditation Council is an autonomous body established by the University Commission of India (UGC) to assess and accredit institutions of higher education in the country. It lay special emphasis on evaluating the quality of higher education in India. NAAC has introduced new a methodology to assess and accredit the higher education institutions in India. In the first step, the institution is required to seek Institutional Eligibility for Quality Assessment (IEQA) and the second step is the assessment and accreditation of the institute under the grades A, B, C for accredited institutions: and D for those which are not accredited. NAAC has identified seven criteria for assessment procedure: Curricular aspects, Teaching-learning and evaluation, Research, Consultancy and extension, Infrastructure and learning resources, Student support and progression, Governance and leadership and Innovative practices.

8. NBA (National Board of Accreditation)

National Board of Accreditation, India was established by AICTE as an autonomous body under section 10(u) of AICTE act, 1994 for periodic evaluations of technical institutions and programmes basis according to specified norms and standards as recommended by AICTE council. It is the only authorized body in India entrusted with the task of undertaking accreditation of technical education programmes. From 7th January 2010, NBA came into existence as an autonomous body with the objective of Assurance of Quality and Relevance of Education, especially of the programmes in professional and technical disciplines, i.e., Engineering and Technology, Management, Architecture, Pharmacy and Hospitality, through the mechanism of accreditation of programmes offered by technical institutions. It has received 2 awards: Golden Peacock Eco Innovation Award 2013, for the eNBA Project and Best Education Project - Silver Award.

9. NIRF (National Institutional Ranking Framework)

National Institutional Ranking Framework is a methodology adopted by the Ministry of Human Resource development (MHRD), Government of India, to rank all institutions of higher education in India. NIRF was set up to identify the broad parameters for ranking various universities and institutions that are: Teaching, learning and resources, Research and professional practices, graduation outcomes, outreach and inclusivity and perception.

10. AIMA (All India Management Association)

With the active support of Government of India and Industry, All India Management Association was created in 1957 as an apex body of professional management. It is a non-lobbying organisation, working closely with industry, Government, academia and students to further the cause of the management profession in India. It is a federation of Local Management Associations (LMAs). AIMA also brings to the Indian managers, the best management practices and techniques through numerous foreign collaborations with professional bodies and institutions.

11. BCI (Bar Council of India)

The Bar Council of India is a statutory body established under the section 4 of advocates Act 1961 that regulates the legal practice and legal education in India. It also grants recognition to Universities whose degree in law will serve as qualification for enrollment as an advocate. It performs certain representative functions by protecting the rights, privileges, and interests of advocates and through the creation of funds for providing financial assistance to organise welfare schemes for them. It prescribes standards of professional conduct, etiquettes, and exercises disciplinary jurisdiction over the bar. To practice law, it is mandatory to pass All India Bar Examination that is conducted by BCI since April 10, 2010. This entrance examination is held biannually in which a candidate can appear any number of times. After clearing this entrance examination every advocate is entitled to a Certified Practice of Law throughout India.

12. DCI (Dental Council of India)

The Dental Council of India is a statutory body incorporated under The Dentist Act, 1948 to *regulate dental education and the profession* throughout India that is financed by the Ministry of Health and Family Welfare and through the local state dental councils. Main objectives of DCI is to maintain uniform standards of dental education in India, regulate the curriculum in the training of dentists, dental hygienists, and dental mechanics and to regulate the level of examinations and qualifications. As per a bill introduced in the Parliament of India, Medical regulatory bodies like The Dental Council of India, Nursing Council of India and Pharmacy Council of India are proposed to dissolve and replaced with a common Statutory Body known as National Commission for Human resources for Health.

13. DEC (Distance Education Council)

Distance Education Council is responsible for the promotion and coordination of the Open University and distance education system and for determination of its standards based in New Delhi, India. It was constituted under the Indira Gandhi National Open University Act, 1985. It tries to promote an innovative system of University level education that has flexible and open methods and pace of learning, combination of courses, eligibility for enrolment and age of entry. It also advises the State Government, universities, and other concerned agencies on their proposals to set up open universities or to introduce programmes of distance education.It appoints Review Committees periodically, which study and assess the performance of the open universities/distance education institutions in its network. But in June 2013, DEC was taken over by the University Grants Commission by establishing Distance Education Bureau (DEB) to govern the distance education programmes in India.

14. NIELIT (National Institute of Electronics and Information Technology) AKADOEACC (Department of Electronics and Accreditation of Computer Courses)

National Institute of Electronics and Information Technology (NIELIT), earlier known as the DOEACC Society, is an autonomous scientific society under the administrative control of Ministry of Electronics and Information Technology of the Government of India. It is also one of the National Examination Body, which accredits institutes/organisations for conducting courses in IT in the non-formal sector. At present, it has 35 offices with its headquarters in New Delhi. It has acquired very good expertise in IT training, through its wide repertoire of causes, ranging from O Level (Foundation), A Level (Advance Diploma), B Level (MCA equivalent), C Level (M-Tech level), IT literacy courses such as CCC (Course on Computer Concept), BCC (Basic Computer Course) and other such long term and short term course in the non-formal sector like courses on Information Security, ITeS-BPO(Customer Care/Banking), Computer Hardware Maintenance (CHM-O/A level), Bio-Informatics(BI-O/A/B level), ESDM etc., besides, high end courses offered by NIELIT Centers at Post-Graduate level (M.Tech) in Electronics Design and Technology, Embedded Systems etc. which are not normally offered by Universities/ Institutions in the formal sector, in association with the respective state Universities.

15. INC (Indian Nursing Council)

The Indian Nursing Council is a national regulatory body for nurses and nurse education in India formed by the Central Government under section 3(1) of the Indian Nursing Council Act, 1947 of the Indian parliament. Their function is to establish and monitor a uniform standard of nursing education for nurse midwife, Auxiliary Nurse- Midwives and health visitors by doing an inspection of the institutions, promote research in nursing and to improve the quality of nursing education. As per a bill introduced in the Parliament of India, Medical regulatory bodies like The Dental Council of India, Nursing Council of India and Pharmacy Council of India are proposed to dissolve and replaced with a common Statutory Body known as National Commission for Human resources for Health.

16. MCI (Medical Council of India)

The Medical Council of India is a statutory body for establishing uniform and high standards of medical education in India. It grants recognition of medical qualifications, gives accreditation to medical schools, grants registration to medical practitioners, and monitors medical practice in India. But recently states has approved the proposal of NITI

(National Institution for Transforming India) Aayog to replace Medical Council of India (MCI) with a statutory body known as the National Medical Commission.As per a bill introduced in the Parliament of India, Medical regulatory bodies like The Dental Council of India, Nursing Council of India and Pharmacy Council of India are proposed to dissolve and replaced with a common Statutory Body known as National Commission for Human resources for Health.

17. NCTE (National Council for Teacher Education)

National Council for Teacher Education is a statutory body of Indian government set up under the National Council for Teacher Education Act in 1995 to formally oversee standards, procedures and processes in the Indian education system. The main objective of the NCTE is to achieve planned and coordinated development of the teacher education system throughout the country, the regulation and proper maintenance of Norms and Standards in the teacher education system and for matters connected therewith.

18. PCI (Pharmacy Council of India)

Pharmacy Council of India is the statutory body of government of India constituted under the Pharmacy Act, 1948 on 4 March 1948. It is constituted by central government every five years.The objectives of the PCI is to regulate the pharmacy education in the Country for the purpose of registration as a pharmacist under the Pharmacy Act and regulate the profession and practice of pharmacy. Recently as per a bill introduced in the Parliament of India, Medical regulatory bodies like The Dental Council of India, Nursing Council of India and Pharmacy Council of India are proposed to dissolve and replaced with a common Statutory Body known as National Commission for Human resources for Health.

19. VCI (Veterinary Council of India)

Established under the Ministry of Agriculture of the Government of India in 1984, the Veterinary Council of India is a statutory body which regulates veterinary practice in India. The council is governed by the Indian Veterinary Council Act, 1984 and receives 100 per cent grants-in-aid from the Department of Animal Husbandry and Dairying, Ministry of Agriculture of Government of India under a Plan Scheme Namely Professional Efficiency Development for undertaking the activities of the Council.

20. NCHRH (National Council for Human Resource in Health)

To regulate health education there will be a new regulatory agency in India by enforcement of a new bill being tabled in the Parliament of India. The Ministry of Health and Family Welfare has approved the revised draft for the proposed NCHRH Bill which will be an overarching body for the health sector. There will be a common MBBS entrance test (single PMT)National Eligibility and Entrance Test -UG replacing the over 17 All India Pre Medical Test(PMTs) conducted all over the country for over 35,000 undergraduate seats.As per a bill introduced in the Parliament of India, Medical regulatory bodies like The Dental Council of India, Nursing Council of India and Pharmacy Council of India are proposed to dissolve and replaced with a common Statutory Body known as National Commission for Human resources for Health.

Appendix - 2

Universities, Colleges, Institutes offering Management Courses through Distance, Correspondence and Open Learning Modes

1. Andhra University, Vishakhapatnam
2. Acharya Nagarjuna University, Guntur
3. Osmania University, Hyderabad
4. Sri Krishnadevaraya University, Anantapur
5. University of Hyderabad
6. GITAM University, Vishakhapatnam
7. Rayalseema University, Kurnool
8. Assam Don Bosco University, Guwahati
9. Patna University, Patna
10. All India Management Association (AIMA)
11. Institute of Rail Transport
12. TECNIA Institute of Advanced Studies, Rohini
13. Institute of Management and Development
14. Guru Jambheshwar University, Hisar
15. Kurukshetra University, Kurukshetra
16. Maharishi Dayanand University, Rohtak
17. Manav Rachna International (Deemed University), Faridabad
18. IILM Institute of Higher Education, Gurugram
19. JK Business School, Gurugram
20. Bengaluru University, Bengaluru
21. Bharatiya Vidya Foundation, Bengaluru
22. Dr. DY Patil University, Pune
23. Narsee Monjee Institute of Management Studies, Mumbai
24. Padamshree Dr. DY Patil University, Navi Mumbai
25. Balaji Institute of Modern Management, Pune
26. Mumbai Education Trust, Mumbai
27. Rashtrabhasha Prachar Samiti, Wardha
28. Symbiosis Centre for Distance Learning, Pune
29. Welingkar Institute of Management Development and Research, Mumbai
30. Indira International Academy, Indira Group of Institutes, Pune
31. PSB Educational Foundation, Pune
32. Indian Institute of Material Management, Navi Mumbai
33. Mahatma Gandhi University, Khana Para
34. Utkal University, Bhubaneswar
35. Asian School of Business Management, Bhubaneswar
36. Pondicherry University, Puducherry
37. Lovely Professional University, Phagwara
38. Punjabi University, Patiala

39. NIMS University, Jaipu
40. Jaipur National University, Jaipur
41. Jagan Nath University, Jaipur
42. Bhagwant University, Ajmer
43. Jayoti Vidyapeeth Women's University, Jaipur
44. Sikkim Manipal University, Gangtok
45. EIILM University, Jorethang
46. Bharathidasan University, Tiruchirapalli
47. Madurai Kamaraj University, Madurai
48. Karpagam University, Coimbatore
49. University of Madras, Chennai
50. Vinayaka Mission's University, Salem
51. Alagappa University, Karaikudi
52. St. Peter's University, Chennai
53. Mother Teresa Women's University, Kudaikanal
54. Confederation of Indian Industry of Logistics, Chennai
55. Meenakshi Academy of Higher Education and Research, Chennai
56. ICFAI University, Agartala
57. U.P. Rajarshi Tandon Open University, Allahabad
58. Allahabad Agricultural Institute (Deemed University), Allahabad
59. Dayalbagh Educational Institute (Deemed University, Agra
60. Swami Vivekananda Subharti University, Meerut
61. NIMT, Greater Noida
62. IMT Distance and Open Learning Institute, Ghaziabad
63. University of Petroleum and Energy Studies, Dehradun
64. ICFAI University, Dehradun
65. Netaji Subhas Open University, Kolkata

Appendix - 3

Times Top 100 B Schools

No.	INSTITUTE/ B-SCHOOL
1.	Indian Institute of Management, Kolkata
2.	XLRI - Xavier School Of Management, Jamshedpur
3.	SP Jain Institute of Management and Research, Mumbai
4.	Management Development Institute, Gurugram
5.	Indian Institute of Management, Kozhikode
6.	Indian Institute of Management, Indore
7.	Indian Institute of Foreign Trade, Delhi
8.	Symbiosis Institute of Business Management, Pune
9.	Amity Business School, Amity University, Noida
10.	Symbiosis Centre for Management and Human Resource Development, Pune
11.	Institute of Rural Management, Anand
12.	Sri Balaji Society (BIMM, BITM, BIIB, BIMHRD), Pune
13.	National Institute of Industrial Engineering (NITIE), Mumbai
14.	Vinod Gupta School of Management - Indian Institute of Technology, Kharagpur
15.	ITM Business School, Mumbai
16.	ICFAI Business School (IBS), Hyderabad
17.	School of Management - SRM University, Chennai
18.	Institute of Management Studies (IMS), Ghaziabad
19.	SCMS Cochin School of Business, Cochin
20.	Pune Institute of Business Management (PIBM), Pune
21.	SIES College of Management Studies, Mumbai
22.	KJ Somaiya Institute of Management Studies and Research, Mumbai
23.	Prin. LN Welingkar Institute of Management Development and Research, Mumbai
24.	Department of Management Studies - Indian Institute of Technology, Chennai
25.	International School of Business and Media (ISB&M), Pune
26.	Shailesh J Mehta School of Management-Indian Institute of Technology, Mumbai
27.	KIIT School of Management, KIIT University, Bhubaneswar
28.	Indus Business Academy, Bengaluru
29.	VIT Business School, VIT University, Vellore
30.	MIT School of Management, Pune
31.	Institute of Public Enterprise, Hyderabad
32.	Faculty of Management Studies, Manav Rachna International University, Faridabad
33.	Apeejay School Of Management, Delhi
34.	Fortune Institute of International Business, Delhi
35.	Faculty of Management Studies - Maharaja Sayajirao University of Baroda, Vadodara
36.	International Institute of Management Studies , Pune
37.	ITM Business School, Chennai
38.	GLA University , Institute of Business Management, Mathura

39. Rajagiri Centre for Business Studies, Cochin
40. Universal Business School, Mumbai
41. MIT School of Technology Management, Pune
42. Galgotias University , School of Business, Greater Noida
43. Jagan Institute Of Management Studies, Rohini, Delhi
44. Sharda University, Greater Noida
45. Bengal Institute of Business Studies, Kolkata
46. Management Institute for Leadership and Excellence (MILE), Pune
47. DC School of Management and Technology, Pullikkanam
48. Jagannath International Management School, Kalkaji, Delhi
49. IIEBM Indus Business School, Pune
50. Prestige Institute of Management, Gwalior
51. Hindustan University, School of Management, Chennai
52. Quantum School of Business, Roorkee
53. International School of Management Excellence, Bengaluru
54. NL Dalmia Institute of Management Studies and Research, Mumbai
55. AIMS School Business (AIMS Institute), Bengaluru
56. Nehru College of Management, Coimbatore
57. Gandhi Institute of Management Studies, Rayagada
58. Gitam Institute of Management, Vishakhapatnam
59. Aurora Business School, Hyderabad
60. Suryadatta Institute of Management, Pune
61. Indian Institute of Management, Kashipur
62. Sinhgad Business School, Pune
63. Indian Institute of Management, Shillong
64. Lotus Business School, Pune
65. Institute of Technology and Science, Ghaziabad
66. Sai Balaji International Institute of Management Sciences, Pune
67. MIT College of Management, Pune
68. SRMS International Business School, Lucknow
69. Faculty of Management Science, Shri Ram Murti Smarak College of Engineering and Technology, Bareilly
70. Institute of Business Management and Research - IPS Academy, Indore
71. Institute Of Management and Information Science, Bhubaneswar
72. Durgadevi Saraf Institute of Management Studies, Mumbai
73. Indian Institute of Knowledge Management, Chennai
74. Smt. Kashibai Navale Sinhgad School of Business Management (SKNSSBM), Pune
75. School of Management - Dr. DY Patil University, Mumbai
76. MS Ramaiah Institute of Management, Bengaluru
77. Kanpur Institute of Technology, Kanpur
78. Apeejay Institute of Management Technical Campus, Jalandhar
79. Accurate Institute of Management and Technology, Greater Noida
80. Sandip Institute of Technology and Research Center, Nashik
81. Atharva Institute of Management Studies, Mumbai
82. National Academy of Event Management and Development (NAEMD), Mumbai
83. Unique Institute of Management and Technology, Ghaziabad

84. IIMT College of Engineering Department of Management, Greater Noida
85. IES Management College and Research Centre, Mumbai
86. ABV - Indian Institute of Information Technology and Management, Gwalior
87. Sinhgad institute of Business Administration and Computer Applications, Pune
88. Vignana Jyothi Institute of Management, Hyderabad
89. Vivekanand Education Society's Institute of Management Studies and Research, Mumbai
90. Sou. Sushila Danchand Ghodawat Charitable Trust's Sanajay Ghodawat Group of Institutions, Kolhapur
91. Dhruva College of Management, Hyderabad
92. MM Institute of Management, MM University, Ambala
93. Measi Institute of Management, Royapeeth
94. NBN Sinhgad School of Management Studies (NBNSSOMS), Pune
95. St Joseph's Degree and PG College, Hyderabad
96. International School of Management, Patna
97. Department of Management Studies - Indian School of Mines, Dhanbad
98. SCMS School of Technology and Management, Cochin
99. Army Institute of Management, Kolkata
100. Institute for Technology and Management, Bengaluru

Appendix - 4
Top B-Schools in India—CSR (2018)

1. Ranking of Top Government B-Schools

1. Indian Institute of Foreign Trade, Qutab Institutional Area, New Delhi
2. Faculty of Management Studies (FMS), Delhi University, Delhi
3. Department of Management Studies, IIT Delhi, Hauz Khas, New Delhi
4. Indian Institute of Management Tiruchirappalli, Trichy, Tamil Nadu
5. National Institute of Industrial Engineering Mumbai, Maharashtra
6. Vinod Gupta School of Management, Kharagpur,West Bengal
7. Jamnalal Bajaj Institute of Management Studies (JBIMS), Mumbai, Maharashtra
8. Institute of Public Enterprise, Hyderabad, Telangana
9. Department of Management Studies, National Institute of technology Tiruchirappalli, Tamil Nadu
10. Bharathidasan Institute of Management, Tiruchirappalli, Tamil Nadu
11. Vaikunth Mehta National Institute of Cooperative Management, Pune, Maharashtra
12. Department of Management Studies, IIT (ISM), Dhanbad, Jharkhand
13. Kerala Institute of Co-operative Management, Thiruvananthapuram, Kerala
14. M. S. Patel Institute, Faculty of Management Studies, Vadodara, Gujarat
15. Institute of Management in Kerala Trivandrum, Kerala

2. Ranking of Supreme B-Schools

1. XLRI - Xavier School of Management, Jamshedpur, Jharkhand
2. Management Development Institute, Gurugram, Haryana
3. Institute of Management Technology, Ghaziabad, Uttar Pradesh
4. International Management Institute, Qutab Institutional Area, New Delhi
5. T.A. Pai Management Institute (TAPMI), Manipal, Karnataka

3. Ranking of Top Leading B-Schools of Super Excellence

1. K. J. Somaiya Institute of Management Studies and Research, Mumbai, Maharashtra
2. Xavier Institute of Management, Xavier University, Bhubaneswar, Odisha
3. Institute of Management, Nirma University, Ahmedabad, Gujarat
4. Symbiosis Centre for Management and Human Resource Development, Pune, Maharashtra
5. Goa Institute of Management, Sattari, Goa
6. Xavier Institute of Management and Entrepreneurship, Bengaluru, Karnataka
7. IBS, ICFAI Business School, Mumbai, Maharashtra
8. Symbiosis Institute of Management Studies (SIMS), Pune, Maharashtra
9. Loyola Institute of Business Administration (LIBA), Chennai, Tamil Nadu
10. Symbiosis Institute of Operations Management Nashik, Maharashtra
11. Lal Bahadur Shastri Institute of Management, Dwarka, New Delhi
12. PSG Institute of Management (PSG College of Technology), Coimbatore, Tamil Nadu
13. Institute of Management technology, Nagpur, Maharashtra

4. Ranking of Top B-Schools of Super Excellence

1. Eastern Institute for Integrated Learning in Management, Kolkata, West Bengal
2. ICFAI Business School, Pune, Maharashtra
3. Rajagiri Centre for Business Studies, Kochi, Kerala
4. ICFAI Business School (IBS), Gurugram, Haryana
5. IFIM Business School, Bengaluru, Karnataka
6. ICFAI Business School, Bengaluru, Karnataka
7. Indian Business Academy (Formerly, Indian Business Academiy), Bengaluru, Karnataka
8. Shri Dharmasthala Manjunatheshwara Institute for Management Development (SDMIMD), Mysore, Karnataka
9. Jagan Institute of Management Studies, Rohini, Delhi
10. Institute of Management Studies, Ghaziabad, Uttar Pradesh
11. School of Petroleum Management, Pandit Deendayal Petroleum University, Gandhinagar, Gujarat
12. Jaipuria Institute of Management, Noida, Uttar Pradesh
13. Jaipuria Institute of Management, Lucknow, Uttar Pradesh
14. Symbiosis Institute of Business Management, Bengaluru, Karnataka
15. Institute for Technology and Management, Navi Mumbai, Maharashtra
16. Fortune Institute of International Business (FIIB), Fortune Institute of International Business (FIIB),
17. Siva Sivani Institute of Management, Secunderabad, Telangana
18. Symbiosis Institute of Telecom Management, Pune, Maharashtra
19. SCMS Cochin School of Business, Cochin, Kerala
20. Institute of Management Technology, Hyderabad, Telangana
21. IIHMR University, Jaipur, Rajasthan
22. Apeejay School of Management, Dwarka, NewDelhi
23. GITAM School of International Business, Visakhapatnam, Andhra Pradesh
24. Jagannath International Management School, Kalkaji, New Delhi

5. Ranking of Top B-Schools of Eminence

1. Symbiosis Centre for Information Technology, Pune, Maharashtra
2. ICFAI Business School, Kolkata, West Bengal
3. Jaipuria Institute of Management, Jaipur, Rajasthan
4. Institute of Rural Management, Jaipur, Rajasthan
5. Institute of Technology and Science, Ghaziabad, Uttar Pradesh
6. Bharati Vidyapeeth's Institute of Management Studies and Research, Navi Mumbai, Maharashtra
7. International School of Management Excellence, Bengaluru, Karnataka
8. G. L. Bajaj Institute of Management and Research, Greater Noida, Uttar Pradesh
9. Acharya Bengaluru B School, Bengaluru, Karnataka
10. International Management Institute, Bhubaneswar, Odisha
11. Symbiosis Institute of Business Management, Hyderabad, Telangana
12. SGPC's Guru Nanak Institute Management Studies, Mumbai, Maharashtra
13. Balaji Institute of Modern Management (BIMM),
14. Prestige Institute of Management and Research, Indore, Madhya Pradesh
15. IBS (ICFAI Business School), Ahhedabad, Gujrat

16. Balaji Institute of Management and Human Resource Development, Pune, Maharashtra
17. Vignana Jyothi Institute of Management, Hyderabad, Telangana
18. Jagan Institute of Management Studies, Jaipur, Rajasthan
19. Balaji Institute of International Business (BIIB), Pune, Maharashtra
20. Symbiosis Institute of Computer Studies and Research, Pune, Maharashtra
21. International School of Information and Management, Jaipur, Rajasthan
22. ICFAI Business School, Dehradun, Uttarakhand
23. Institute of Management Studies, Noida, Uttar Pradesh
24. School of Management Studies, Bannari Amman Institute of Technology, Erode, Tamil Nadu
25. Vivekanand Education Society's Institute of Management Studies and Research, Mumbai, Maharashtra

6. **Ranking of Outstanding B-Schools of Excellence**

1. SRM School of Management, Chennai, Tamil Nadu
2. MIT School of Telecom Management, Pune, Maharashtra
3. JK Business School, Gurugram, Haryana
4. International School of Business and Media, Pune, Maharashtra
5. Maharishi Markandeshwar Institute of Management, Mullana-Ambala, Haryana
6. Kirloskar Institute of Advanced Management Studies, Harihar, Karnataka
7. Kalinga University, Naya Raipur, Chhattisgarh
8. Prestige Institute of Management, Gwalior, Madhya Pradesh
9. Suryadatta Institute of Management and Mass Communication (SIMMC), Pune, Maharashtra
10. Sona School of Management, Salem, Tamil Nadu
11. School of Management, MAHE, Manipal, Karnataka
12. Balaji Institute of Telecom and Management, Pune, Maharashtra
13. Jaipuria Institute of Management, Ghaziabad, Uttar Pradesh
14. Rungta College of Engineering and Technology, Bhilai, Chhattisgarh
15. NERIM Group of Institutions, Guwahati, Assam
16. Lala Lajpatrai Institute of Management, Mumbai, Maharashtra
17. Kristu Jayanti College Autonomous, Bengaluru, Karnataka
18. School of Business Studies, Shobhit University, Meerut, Uttar Pradesh
19. Dr. V. N. Bedekar Institute of Management Studies, Thane West, Maharashtra
20. Nehru College of Management, Coimbatore, Tamil Nadu
21. Jaipuria Institute of Management, Indore, Madhya Pradesh
22. School of Management, Vel Tech Rangarajan Dr. Sagunthala R&D Institute of Science and Technology, Chennai, Tamil Nadu
23. IPS Academy, Institute of Business Management and Research, Indore, Madhya Pradesh
24. Veltech High Tech Dr. Rangarajan Dr. Sukanthala Engineering College, Chennai, Tamil Nadu
25. Accurate Institute of Management and Technology, Greater Noida, Uttar Pradesh
26. Bhavan's Centre for Communication and Management, Bhubaneshwar, Odisha
27. Institute for Technology and Management, Chennai, Tamil Nadu
28. Institute of Management and Information Science, Bhubaneswar, Odisha

7. **Ranking of Top B-Schools of Excellence**

1. St. Aloysius Institute of Management and Information Technology, St. Aloysius College (Autonomous), Mangalore, Karnataka
2. D. C. School of Management and Technology, Idukki, Kerala
3. School of Business, Galgotias University, Greater Noida, Uttar Pradesh
4. Saintgits Institute of Management, Kottayam, Kerala
5. IIEBM, Indus Business School, Pune, Maharashtra
6. Rajarambapu Institute of Technology, Rajaramnagar, Sangli, Maharashtra
7. Asian Business School , Noida, Uttar Pradesh
8. School of Management, Presidency University, Bengaluru, Karnataka
9. Sasmira's Institute of Management Studies and Research, Mumbai, Maharashtra
10. Presidency College, Bengaluru, Karnataka
11. Chandigarh Business School of Administration, Mohali, Punjab
12. St. Joseph's Institute of Management, Tiruchirappalli, Tamil Nadu
13. Durgadevi Saraf Institute of Management Studies, Mumbai, Maharashtra
14. Gandhi Institute of Management Studies, Gunupur, Odisha
15. Sinhgad Business School, Pune, Maharashtra
16. GNIOT MBA Institute, Greater Noida, Uttar Pradesh
17. Prestige Institute of Management, Dewas, Madhya Pradesh
18. ITM Business School (Warangal Institute of Management), Warangal, Telengana
19. Karnataka Law Society's Institute Of Management Education and Research, Belagavi, Karnataka
20. C K Shah Vijapurwala Institute of Management, Vadodara, Gujarat
21. Tilak Raj Chadha Institute of Management and Technology, Yamuna Nagar, Haryana
22. Sterling Institute of Management Studies, Navi Mumbai, Maharashtra
23. Indian Institute of Finance (IIF), Greater Noida, Uttar Pradesh.

8. **Ranking of Promising B-Schools**

1. Ajay Kumar Garg Institute of Management, Ghazibad, Uttar Pradesh
2. Sagar Institute of Research and Technology, Bhopal, Madhya Pradesh
3. Reva University, School of Management Studies, Bengaluru, Karnataka
4. St. Joseph's Degree and PG College (Autonomous), Hyderabad, Telangana
5. Dr. D. Y. Patil Institute of Management and Research, Pune, Maharashtra
6. Ramaiah Institute of Management Studies, Bengaluru, Karnataka
7. Institute of Business Management, GLA University, Mathura, Uttar Pradesh
8. APIIT SD, Panipat, Haryana
9. Amrapali Institute of Management and Computer Applications, Haldwani, Uttarakhand
10. RMD Sinhgad School of Management Studies, Pune, Maharashtra
11. Chetan Business School, Hubli, Karnataka
12. Nehru Institute Of Management Studies, Coimbatore, Tamil Nadu
13. Om Kothari Institute of Management and Research, Kota, Rajasthan
14. Vidyasagar Institute of Management, Bhopal, Madhya Pradesh

References

AICTE (2018). *Model Curriculum for Management Programme (MBA & PGDM)*

Ankush, M (2012). Management Education: Recent Trends, Challenges and Opportunities. *University News,* 50 (6)

Bansal etal (2012). Bridging the Research – Practice Gap. *Academy of Management Prespectives,* 26 (1)

Bhattacharya, A (2010). Management of Indian Management Education, *Economic & Political Weekly,* June 12-18

Balaji, R (2013). Trends, Issues and Challenges in Management Education. *International Journal of Innovative Research in Science, Engineering and Technology,* 2

Bowonder and Rao, SL (2005). *Management Education in India, its Evolution and Some Contemporary Issues.* AIMA/CME

Choudary, Sarita (2011). Emerging Issues in Management Education in India. *International Journal of Business and Management Research,* (3)

Edwin Christopher (2015). Management Education: Issues, Challenges and Opportunities in India. *Asian Journal of Management Research,* 6 (1)

Hugar S.S (2001). *Challenges before Business Education.* New Delhi: Atlantic Publishers and Distributors.

Indian Institutes of Management (2019). *Competition Success Review.* (Feb. 2019)

Jagdishbhai Patel (2016). The Changing Face of Management Education: Challenges for Tomorrow. *Indian Streams Research Journal,* 1 (6)

Dayal, I (2002). Developing Management Education in India. *Journal of Management Research,* 2 (2)

Ganguly, P (1998). Are our Management Institutes Responsible Enough, *Indian Management* 1998, August

GFM (2007). *The Global Management Education Landscape: Shaping the Future of Business School*

Ghoshal, S (2005). Bad Management Theories are Destroying Good Management Practices *Academy of Management Learning and Education,* 4 (1)

Goutam, Saha, G (2012). Management Education in India: Issues & Concerns. *Journal of Information, Knowledge and Research in Business Management and Administration,* 2 (1)

Global Foundation for Management Education (2007). *The Global Management Education Landscape: Shaping the Future of Business Schools*

Goe, Sanchita (2012). Challenges and Opportunities in Management Education in India. *Viewpoint,* 3(1)

Gopinath, C (1998). Alternative Approuches to Indigenous Management in India, *Management International Review,* 38(3)

Kaul, N (2011). Management Education in India: A Case Study. *Asian Journal of Management Research,* 2(1)

Khurana, R and Nohria, N (2008). It is Time to make Management a True Profession. *Harvard Business Reviews.* 86 (1)

Khurana, R (2008). *MBA: Review, Managing Management Education.* The ICFAI University Press.

Kumar, N (2011). Taking Stock of Indian Management Research, *The Economic Times*, (February 7)

Kumar, S and Dash, MK (2011). Management Education in India: Trends, Issues and Implications. *Research Journal of International Studies*. (18)

Kumar, M and Shweta (2011). Management Education in India: Issues & Challenges. *Journal of Management & Public Policy*. 3(1)

Kumar, N (2011). Taking Stock of Management Research. *The Economic Tiems*, (2011, Feb. 7)

Khandai, Sujata (2000). Dismal State of Management Education. *Indian Management*, 2000 January

Maharshi, N and Arora, L (2013). Management Education in India: From Challenges to Opportunities. *Asia Pacific Journal of Management &Entrepreneurship Research*, 2(1)

Mannivannan, DG (2006). A New Model for B-School Grading. *Indian Management*, February 2006.

MBA : The Most Coveted Specialisation, *Competition Success Review*. (2019 March)

Misra, S and Chand, PS (Eds) (1999). *Institution Building. An International Perspective on Management Education*. New Delhi: Macmillan

Mishra at al (2015). Indian Ehtos and Future Management Education. *University News*, 53 (14)

Mulla, Z R (2007). Business School Research in India: Seeking the why of Management. *Management and Labour Studies*, 32 (2)

Narendran, R and Narendran, V (2000). Changing Scenario of Management Education. *University News*, 38 (50).

Neelam Sheoliha (2012). Restructuring Management Education Today, For Better Tomorrow. *ZENITH International Journal of Multidisipilnary, Research*, 2(2).

Ojha, AK (2005). Management Education in India: Protecting it from the Rankings onslaught. *Decision*, 32 (2)

Pathania, KS and Anuradha Pathak (2018). Business Schools in India: Issues for Introspection. *University New;* 56 (43).

Patel, B A (2012). Business Management Education in India: Evaluation Challenges and Future Actions. *Journal of Advances in Developments Research*, 3 (1)

Philips, J (2009). *Business Education in India: Ringside View*, Bengaluru XIME

Rahul Mishra (2010). Challenges for Indian B-Schools. *Business Standard. 18*

Ranjana, MV (2017). Educational Transformations: What B-Schools Can give to Business? *University News*, 55 (50)

Ritika Mahajan Nangia and Vinay Sharma (2012). Management Education Landscape in India: Issues, Challenges and Strategies. *AIMA Journal of Management and Research*, 6 (4)

Rahul Mishra (2010). Challenges for Indian B-Schools. *Business Standard*, September 18.

Rajesh Babu, R (2017). *Envisioning the Future of Indian Management Education*. Singapore: Springer

Rao, SL (2005). *Report of the Working Groups on Management Education formed by National Knowledge Committee.*

Sanchita and Goel, MM (2012). Challenges and Opportunities in Management Education in India. *Viewpoint*, 3 (1)

Sankaran, Kand Joshi; G.V (2016). Autonomy for Excellence in Higher Education in India. *Nittee Management Review*, 10 (2)

Saha, GG (2007). Management Education in India: Issues and Concerns. *Journal of Information, Knowledge & Research in Business Management and Administration*? 2 (2)

Satyanarayana, P and Lakshmi Mantha (2018). Management Education in India: Issues and Concerns. *University News*. 56 (20)

Sinha, Dharmi (2004).*Management Education in India: Perspective and* Challenges Hyderabad: ICFAI Press

Shetty, NS (2006). Management Education in India: Challenges of Globalisation: *Souvenir, Poorna Prajna Institute of Management,* Udipi

Shubhendu, S (2013). Management Education in India: Issues and Concerns. *International Journal of Education and Learning,* 2 (2)

Srivastava, SS (2002). *Development of Management Education in India.* New Delhi: Anmol Publications

Swetha and Manoj, K (2011). Management Education in India: Issues & Challenges. *Journal of Management and Public policy,* 3 (1)

Thanuja, BM and Mohapatra, S (2006). IIMs Face Shortage. *The Economic Times,* (Jan. 11)

Thomas, H (2010). Impactful Management Research: The Importance fo Finding the Voice of Practice in Management Research. In *From Challenge to Change: Business Schools in the wake of Financial Crisis*. (A Competition of Essays Put Together by Global Foundation for Management Education)

UGC Regulations on Multiple Accreditation Agencies. UGC Website (www.ugc.ac.in) (2018)

Varma, A and Budhwar, P (2012). International Human Resources Management in the India's Center. *Journal of World Business,* 47 (2)

Vijay Kannan (2008). Business Schools in India: Current Challenges and Future Opportunities. *Decision Line,* October, 2008.

Vijay Krishna (2000). Installing Quality in Management Education. *Indian Management,* June, 2000.

Index